SARDINIA

TRAVEL GUIDE

2023-2024

"Sardinia Uncovered: Your Ultimate Handbook to Exploring Beaches, Culture, Cuisine, practical guide to Mediterranean vacation"

SARA KHAN

COPYRIGHT

Contents

ABOUT THE BOOK

SARDINIA UNVEILED!

Are you ready to embark on a captivating journey to the stunning island of Sardinia, where azure waters, ancient ruins, and vibrant culture intertwine to create an unforgettable experience?

Introducing "Sardinia Unveiled," your perfect guide meticulously crafted to unveil the treasures of this Italian paradise.

WHAT AWAITS YOU WITHIN THESE PAGES

1. COASTAL WONDERS: Explore the breathtaking beauty of Sardinia's coastlines, from the pristine beaches of Costa Smeralda to the rugged cliffs of Cala Gonone, immersing yourself in the mesmerizing Mediterranean landscape.

2. ANCIENT MYSTERIES: Delve into the island's rich history as you uncover the secrets of ancient nuraghe towers, walk through Roman ruins in Nora, and step back in time in the medieval town of Alghero.

3. CULINARY JOURNEY: Indulge in the delectable flavors of Sardinian cuisine, savoring fresh seafood, hearty pasta dishes, and local wines that reflect the island's unique terroir.

4. VIBRANT MARKETS: Immerse yourself in the lively atmosphere of Sardinian markets, from the bustling stalls of Cagliari's Mercato di San Benedetto to the colorful displays of Oristano's Mercato Civico.

5. NATURE'S SPLENDOR: Venture into Sardinia's diverse landscapes, from the dramatic Gola Su Gorropu gorge to the tranquil beauty of the Maddalena Archipelago, experiencing the island's natural wonders.

6. TRADITIONS & FESTIVALS: Witness the vibrant local culture through traditional festivals like Sartiglia and Sant'Efisio, where ancient rituals and modern celebrations come together in a captivating blend.

7. HIDDEN GEMS: Discover off-the-beaten-path treasures, from secluded coves accessible only by boat to charming villages tucked away in the mountains, allowing you to experience the true essence of Sardinia.

8. OUTDOOR PURSUITS: Engage in a plethora of outdoor activities, from hiking the Supramonte range to windsurfing in Porto Pollo, embracing the island's adventurous spirit.

9. ARTISANAL CRAFTS: Explore Sardinia's craftsmanship, from intricate filigree jewelry to handwoven textiles, and learn about the artisans who keep these traditions alive.

10. LOCAL ENCOUNTERS: Immerse yourself in the warmth of Sardinian hospitality by connecting with locals, experiencing their way of life, and gaining insights into the island's soul.

11. PRACTICAL GUIDANCE: Find essential advice on transportation, insider tips, cultural etiquette, and helpful insights to ensure your Sardinian journey is seamless, enjoyable, and culturally respectful.

12. CUSTOMIZED ITINERARIES: Unlock thoughtfully designed itineraries catering to diverse interests and timelines, ensuring you capture the most enchanting facets of this Mediterranean gem.

Grab your copy now, and allow the pages to transport you into an extraordinary expedition through the captivating landscapes of this Italian treasure.

IMPORTANT FACTS ABOUT SARDINIA

Sardinia, the second-largest island in the Mediterranean Sea, is renowned for its rich history, stunning landscapes, and unique culture. Here are some key points about this captivating Italian island:

1. Historical Significance: Sardinia boasts a long and diverse history, with evidence of human habitation dating back to prehistoric times. It has been inhabited by various civilizations, including the Phoenicians, Carthaginians, Romans, Byzantines, and various medieval kingdoms.

2. Breathtaking Landscapes: The island is characterized by its diverse landscapes, ranging from rugged mountains, such as the Gennargentu Range, to picturesque beaches with crystal-clear waters along its extensive coastline.

3. Unique Language and Culture: Sardinia has its own distinct language called Sardinian, which comes in several dialects. The local culture is deeply rooted and showcases influences from its various historical occupiers.

4. Nuragic Civilization: One of Sardinia's most remarkable features is its Nuragic civilization, which existed from around 1800 BCE to 238 BCE. The Nuraghe, ancient stone towers, are iconic symbols of this culture. These mysterious structures are believed to have served as defensive forts, dwellings, or religious sites.

5. Culinary Delights: Sardinian cuisine is celebrated for its unique flavors and ingredients. Roasted meats, locally produced cheeses like Pecorino Sardo, and dishes like "porceddu" (roast suckling pig) are popular. The island is also known for its production of high-quality wines, including Cannonau and Vermentino.

6. Hospitality and Festivals: Sardinians are known for their warm hospitality, which is evident in their traditional festivals and celebrations. One such festival is "Sagra di Sant'Efisio," a colorful procession held in Cagliari each May to honor the patron saint of the island.

7. Environmental Treasures: Sardinia is home to several protected natural areas, including national parks and marine reserves. The island's biodiversity includes unique species of plants and animals, some of which are found nowhere else on Earth.

8. Ancient Megalithic Sites: In addition to Nuragic structures, Sardinia is home to several megalithic sites, including the "Tomba dei Giganti" or Giant's Tomb, massive tombs dating back to prehistoric times.

9. Political and Economic Dynamics: While part of Italy, Sardinia has had movements advocating for increased autonomy and recognition of its unique identity. The island's economy historically relied on agriculture and mining, but it has diversified over the years to include tourism and other sectors.

10. Modern Challenges: Like many regions, Sardinia faces challenges such as maintaining its cultural heritage, preserving its environment, and ensuring sustainable development that benefits its residents.

In summary, Sardinia is a captivating destination that offers a blend of history, culture, natural beauty, and unique traditions. Its distinct identity and breathtaking landscapes make it a place of enduring interest for travelers and scholars alike.

SARDINIA ITINERARIES

7-Day Sardinia Itinerary:
Exploring the Island's Natural Beauty and
Culture

Day 1: Arrival in Cagliari

Begin your Sardinian adventure in the capital city of Cagliari. Explore the historic Castello district with its narrow streets, ancient walls, and panoramic views. Visit the National Archaeological Museum to learn about the island's rich history.

Day 2: Beach Day in Villasimius

Head to the stunning beaches of Villasimius, known for their turquoise waters and white sands. Spend the day relaxing, swimming, and enjoying water sports. Don't miss the scenic Capo Carbonara promontory.

Day 3: Costa Smeralda

Drive north to the glamorous Costa Smeralda. Visit Porto Cervo, a luxury resort town with designer boutiques and upscale restaurants. Enjoy the beautiful beaches like Spiaggia del Principe and explore the rugged coastline.

Day 4: Alghero

Travel to Alghero on the northwest coast. Wander through the charming Old Town with its Catalan influence. Explore Neptune's Grotto, a stunning sea cave, and take a stroll along the historic city walls.

Day 5: Nuragic Sites and Stintino

Discover Sardinia's prehistoric Nuragic civilization at sites like Su Nuraxi in Barumini. In the afternoon, head to Stintino and enjoy La Pelosa Beach, known for its crystal-clear waters and fine sand.

Day 6: Gola Su Gorropu

Embark on a hiking adventure in Gola Su Gorropu, Europe's deepest canyon. The breathtaking scenery and challenging trails make this a memorable experience for nature enthusiasts.

Day 7: Departure

Spend your last morning exploring local markets in Cagliari for souvenirs and traditional Sardinian products before departing.

5-Day Sardinia Itinerary: Coastal Charm and Cultural Gems

Day 1: Cagliari and Nora

Arrive in Cagliari and explore the city's historic sites. In the afternoon, visit the ancient ruins of Nora, an archaeological site by the sea.

Day 2: Charming Villages

Drive to Bosa, a colorful riverside town known for its pastel buildings. Continue to Castelsardo, home to a medieval castle and panoramic views.

Day 3: Alghero and Neptune's Grotto

Travel to Alghero and enjoy the coastal scenery. Explore Neptune's Grotto and stroll through the city's historic center.

Day 4: Costa Paradiso

Discover Costa Paradiso's rugged beauty. Relax on Li Cossi Beach and admire the unique red-rock formations.

Day 5: Departure

Spend your last morning at leisure, perhaps enjoying a final Italian espresso, before departing.

3-Day Sardinia Itinerary: Quick Getaway of Highlights

Day 1: Cagliari Exploration

Arrive in Cagliari and explore the main attractions like Castello district and the National Archaeological Museum.

Day 2: Coastal Beauty

Head to Costa Smeralda, visiting Porto Cervo and soaking in the stunning coastal views.

Day 3: Departure

Visit a local market for some last-minute shopping before departing from Sardinia.

These itineraries offer a glimpse into the diverse experiences that Sardinia has to offer, from pristine beaches to ancient ruins and charming villages. Customize each itinerary based on your interests and enjoy your unforgettable journey on this beautiful Mediterranean island.

INTRODUCTION TO SARDINIA

Welcome to the captivating island of Sardinia, a Mediterranean gem renowned for its breathtaking landscapes, rich history, and vibrant culture. Nestled within the azure waters of the Tyrrhenian Sea, Sardinia beckons with its stunning beaches, rugged mountains, and a tapestry of traditions that have flourished over millennia.

At the heart of Sardinia's allure lies its diverse geography. Sandy shores stretch along its coastline, offering a paradise for sun-seekers and water enthusiasts. Crystal-clear waters invite snorkelers and divers to explore a vibrant underwater world. Inland, the island transforms into a rugged terrain of mountains, valleys, and ancient forests, inviting adventurers to hike, bike, and explore its untamed beauty.

But Sardinia isn't just a visual feast; its history is equally captivating. Traces of ancient civilizations can be found in the mysterious Nuragic ruins that dot the landscape. These prehistoric stone structures, built by the Nuragic people, are shrouded in intrigue, captivating archaeologists and history enthusiasts alike. The island's cultural heritage is also reflected in its festivals, where locals celebrate age-old traditions through music, dance, and gastronomy.

Speaking of gastronomy, Sardinia's culinary scene is a testament to its unique identity. The island's cuisine draws from its geographical diversity, with coastal regions offering delectable seafood dishes, while the interior boasts hearty fare made from locally sourced ingredients. Don't miss the chance to savor specialties like "porceddu," a succulent roasted piglet, or "malloreddus," a delightful pasta shaped like small gnocchi.

Hospitality is deeply ingrained in Sardinian culture, and the warmth of its people is palpable. Engaging with locals offers a glimpse into their traditional way of life and provides an authentic experience that can't be replicated elsewhere.

Whether you're exploring the ancient ruins of Nora, lounging on the pristine beaches of Costa Smeralda, or savoring the flavors of Sardinian cuisine, this island beckons with a unique blend of history, nature, and culture. With a landscape that shifts from vibrant coastal scenes to rugged hinterlands, and a heritage that intertwines modernity with centuries-old traditions, Sardinia stands as a testament to the timeless allure of the Mediterranean.

CHAPTER 1

DISCOVERING SARDINIA

1.1. OVERVIEW OF SARDINIA

Sardinia, the second-largest island in the Mediterranean Sea, is an Italian autonomous region renowned for its stunning landscapes, rich history, and unique culture. Nestled southwest of the Italian peninsula, Sardinia captivates visitors with its diverse terrain, ranging from rugged mountains to pristine beaches.

The island's history dates back thousands of years, marked by the influences of various civilizations. Its strategic location made it a crossroads for Phoenician, Roman, Byzantine, and Spanish rule, all of which left their indelible marks on the architecture, cuisine, and traditions. Sardinia's ancient Nuragic civilization, known for its mysterious stone towers, stands as a testament to its remarkable past.

The island's landscape is characterized by the dramatic Gennargentu mountain range, which dominates the interior. These peaks shelter quaint villages and picturesque towns, showcasing the island's rustic charm. The coastal areas, on the other hand, boast crystal-clear waters and dazzling beaches, making Sardinia a haven for sun-seekers and water sports enthusiasts.

Sardinian culture is a captivating blend of influences, with a language, Sardinian, that differs significantly from Italian. Traditional festivals, like the lively "Sardinian Carnival," celebrate the island's unique identity through colorful costumes and folk dances. Local cuisine is a culinary adventure, featuring dishes like "porceddu" (roast piglet) and "culurgiones" (stuffed pasta), often paired with the robust Sardinian wines.

The island's archaeological wonders include the aforementioned Nuragic towers, mysterious stone structures shrouded in historical intrigue. The UNESCO-listed Su Nuraxi di Barumini is the most famous of these sites. Meanwhile, medieval towns like Alghero showcase Spanish influence, evident in the architecture and even the local Catalan dialect.

Sardinia's natural beauty beckons outdoor enthusiasts. The Golfo di Orosei's limestone cliffs create awe-inspiring gorges and caves, while the Costa Smeralda's turquoise waters and upscale resorts attract international jet-setters. Hiking, biking, and exploring the untouched wilderness are popular activities in Sardinia's numerous nature reserves.

In summary, Sardinia's allure lies in its captivating blend of history, culture, and landscapes. From ancient archaeological sites to pristine beaches, the island offers a diverse range of experiences for those seeking both relaxation and exploration. Its rich heritage and natural wonders make Sardinia a truly remarkable destination in the heart of the Mediterranean.

1.2. HISTORICAL BACKGROUND

Sardinia, an island situated in the Mediterranean Sea, has a rich historical background that spans millennia. Its history has been shaped by a diverse range of civilizations, leaving behind a tapestry of cultural influences and architectural wonders. The island's strategic location made it a desirable target for various powers throughout history.

The earliest known inhabitants of Sardinia were the Nuragic people, who established a unique Bronze Age civilization from around 1800 to 500 BCE. They built distinctive stone towers known as nuraghi, which served as fortified dwellings and cultural symbols. These structures still dot the Sardinian landscape, attesting to the island's ancient heritage.

Over the centuries, Sardinia was conquered by multiple civilizations, including the Phoenicians, Carthaginians, and Romans. The Roman Republic incorporated the island into its territories in 238 BCE, leading to a period of Romanization and the construction of roads, bridges, and aqueducts. Sardinia's agricultural resources and mineral wealth made it a valuable asset to the Roman Empire.

Following the fall of the Western Roman Empire in the 5th century CE, Sardinia experienced successive waves of invasions by Vandals, Byzantines, Arabs, and Pisans. By the 11th century, the island was divided among various competing powers, including the Giudicati, semi-autonomous regions ruled by local judges.

In the late Middle Ages, the Aragonese Crown gained control over Sardinia. This period saw the construction of numerous fortifications and the blending of Catalan-Aragonese traditions with the island's existing culture. The House of Savoy later acquired the island in the 18th century as a result of the War of Spanish Succession, and Sardinia became a part of the Kingdom of Sardinia.

The 19th century brought political changes, with Sardinia playing a pivotal role in the unification of Italy. Cavour, the Prime Minister of Sardinia, collaborated with other Italian states to drive out foreign powers and unite the peninsula into the Kingdom of Italy in 1861. Sardinia retained a degree of autonomy within the new kingdom due to its unique cultural and administrative heritage.

Despite its incorporation into Italy, Sardinia faced economic challenges and emigration during the 20th century. The island's distinct languages and cultures, including Sardinian and Catalan, continued to flourish alongside Italian.

Today, Sardinia is renowned for its stunning landscapes, ancient ruins, and vibrant traditions. Its history is a testament to the resilience of its people and the convergence of diverse civilizations. The legacy of the Nuragic civilization, Roman influence, medieval fortifications, and the struggle for Italian unification have all contributed to the island's fascinating historical tapestry.

1.3. CLIMATE AND WEATHER

Sardinia, the second-largest island in the Mediterranean Sea, experiences a Mediterranean climate characterized by mild, wet winters and hot, dry summers. The island's climate is influenced by its geographical location, proximity to the sea, and surrounding terrain.

During the winter months, which typically span from November to February, Sardinia sees cooler temperatures and increased rainfall. The island's mountainous interior experiences more precipitation than the coastal areas, with the Gennargentu range often covered in snow. Coastal temperatures remain relatively mild, with daytime highs ranging from 10 to 15 degrees Celsius (50 to 59 degrees Fahrenheit).

March to May is characterized by increasing temperatures and a decrease in rainfall. Spring is considered one of the best times to visit Sardinia due to the comfortable weather and blooming landscapes. Daytime temperatures climb to around 18 to 23 degrees Celsius (64 to 73 degrees Fahrenheit).

Summer in Sardinia, from June to September, is the hottest and driest season. Coastal areas experience high temperatures, with average daytime highs ranging from 28 to 32 degrees Celsius (82 to 90 degrees Fahrenheit). The island's interior can become even hotter, with temperatures occasionally exceeding 35 degrees Celsius (95 degrees Fahrenheit). The lack of rainfall during this period leads to a risk of drought and water scarcity.

Autumn arrives in Sardinia around October, bringing cooler temperatures and increasing rainfall. While the island doesn't experience the vibrant fall foliage of more temperate climates, the landscape remains picturesque. The months of September and October are considered a pleasant time to explore Sardinia, as the summer crowds have dissipated, and the weather is still relatively mild.

Sardinia's weather patterns are also influenced by its surrounding seas. The Mediterranean Sea helps to moderate temperatures, preventing extreme temperature fluctuations. Additionally, the island's proximity to North Africa can occasionally lead to the influx of hot, dry winds, known as the Sirocco, which can result in temporary spikes in temperatures.

Climate change is affecting Sardinia, as it is many other regions across the globe. Rising temperatures, changing precipitation patterns, and the potential for more intense and frequent extreme weather events are among the concerns. Such changes could impact Sardinia's ecosystems, agriculture, and water resources.

In conclusion, Sardinia's climate exhibits the classic traits of a Mediterranean climate, with distinct seasons characterized by varying temperatures and rainfall patterns. The island's unique geography and location contribute to its weather patterns, making it a destination that offers a range of experiences throughout the year. However, it's important to remain mindful of the potential impacts of climate change on Sardinia's delicate ecosystem and local communities.

1.4. LANGUAGE AND LOCAL CUSTOMS

Sardinia, an enchanting island located in the Mediterranean Sea, boasts a unique blend of language and local customs that reflect its rich history and cultural diversity. The island's distinct identity is deeply rooted in its linguistic heritage and traditional practices.

Language plays a pivotal role in shaping Sardinian culture. The island is home to the Sardinian language, a Romance language with various dialects. Although Italian is the official language, Sardinian holds a special place in the hearts of the locals. This linguistic diversity is a testament to Sardinia's historical connections to different civilizations, including the Phoenicians, Romans, and Spanish. The Sardinian language acts as a cultural marker, preserving ancient expressions, idioms, and vocabulary that provide insight into the island's past.

Local customs in Sardinia are deeply intertwined with its agrarian history, showcasing a close relationship with the land and the sea. Traditional festivals and celebrations, known as "feste," are essential aspects of Sardinian life. One of the most renowned is the "Sagra di Sant'Efisio," a religious procession that honors the patron saint of the island. During this event, locals wear traditional clothing and showcase equestrian skills, symbolizing their agrarian heritage and equestrian traditions.

Cuisine is another integral part of Sardinian culture. The island's food is a reflection of its natural resources and historical influences. Staples like "pane carasau," a thin, crispy bread, and "culurgiones," handmade stuffed pasta, highlight the island's culinary uniqueness. Sardinians also have a strong tradition of pastoralism, resulting in the production of distinctive cheeses like "pecorino sardo." These culinary customs not only showcase Sardinia's agricultural practices but also underline the significance of communal dining and familial bonds.

In Sardinia, the connection to the land is further evident in its handicrafts. Basket weaving, ceramics, and textiles are popular artisanal traditions that have been passed down through generations. These crafts are often made using local materials, reflecting the island's resourcefulness and commitment to preserving its heritage.

Sardinian society places great emphasis on community and family bonds. The "nuraghi," ancient stone structures unique to Sardinia, serve as powerful symbols of the island's history and collective identity. These structures were once part of a complex network of villages and settlements, reflecting the island's communal lifestyle.

In conclusion, Sardinia's language and local customs encapsulate the island's rich history and cultural diversity. The Sardinian language acts as a linguistic link to the past, while traditional customs, festivals, and cuisine provide insight into the island's agrarian roots and strong sense of community. Through its distinct customs and linguistic heritage, Sardinia proudly stands as a testament to the enduring spirit of its people and their connection to their unique cultural legacy.

1.5. YOUR FIRST TRIP TO SARDINIA

Visiting Sardinia for the first time is an enchanting experience that promises a blend of breathtaking landscapes, rich history, and vibrant culture. This picturesque Italian island, located in the heart of the Mediterranean, boasts stunning beaches, rugged cliffs, and crystal-clear waters that beckon travelers to its shores.

Sardinia's coastline is a paradise for beach lovers. From the famous Costa Smeralda with its glamorous resorts to hidden coves like Cala Goloritzé, there's a beach for every preference. The turquoise waters and fine sand create a relaxing atmosphere that's hard to resist.

Beyond the beaches, Sardinia's interior is a treasure trove of archaeological wonders. The Nuragic civilization, which flourished here over 3,000 years ago, left behind mysterious stone structures known as nuraghe. These ancient towers dot the landscape, offering a glimpse into a fascinating past.

Exploring Sardinian cuisine is a delight for the senses. The island's culinary traditions are a blend of Italian, Spanish, and North African influences. Don't miss out on trying dishes like "porceddu" (roast suckling pig) and "malloreddus" (a type of pasta) served with rich sauces. Pair your meal with a local Cannonau wine for an authentic gastronomic experience.

For those seeking adventure, the island's interior offers hiking opportunities through rugged mountains and lush valleys. The Gennargentu National Park is a prime spot for outdoor enthusiasts, with trails leading to the island's highest peak, Punta La Marmora.

Immersing yourself in Sardinian culture means participating in traditional festivals and events. The "Sagra" food festivals showcase local specialties and are a great way to mingle with the locals. Experience the vibrant "Sardinian Cavalcade," a colorful procession of traditional costumes, music, and dance that celebrates the island's heritage.

Sardinia's charm extends to its welcoming locals, who often share their customs and stories with visitors. Engaging with them can provide a deeper understanding of the island's unique identity and way of life.

In conclusion, a trip to Sardinia offers a captivating blend of natural beauty, history, and culture. Whether you're lounging on its stunning beaches, exploring ancient ruins, indulging in delicious cuisine, or immersing yourself in local traditions, this island will leave an indelible mark on your travel memories.

CHAPTER 2

PLANNING YOUR SARDINIA ADVENTURE

2.1. BEST TIME TO VISIT SARDINIA

The best time to visit Sardinia depends on your preferences and the activities you have in mind. Sardinia, an Italian island in the Mediterranean, experiences a Mediterranean climate with warm summers and mild winters.

Summer (June to August) is the peak tourist season due to its warm temperatures and clear skies. This is an ideal time for beach lovers and water sports enthusiasts. The island's pristine beaches and turquoise waters attract a large number of visitors during these months. However, this popularity also means that the beaches can get crowded, and accommodation prices tend to be higher.

Spring (April to May) and early autumn (September to October) offer a pleasant climate with milder temperatures and fewer crowds. This is a great time for outdoor activities like hiking, exploring historic sites, and enjoying local cuisine. The landscapes are lush, and the weather is generally comfortable for sightseeing.

If you're interested in cultural experiences and want to avoid the peak tourist season, consider visiting during the off-peak months of November to March. During these months, you can explore Sardinia's charming towns, archaeological sites, and museums without the crowds. However, do note that some attractions might have limited operating hours during this time.

Winter (December to February) is the least popular time to visit due to cooler temperatures and the possibility of rain. While the island might not be suitable for beach activities during these months, it can be a unique opportunity to experience Sardinia's local life, traditional festivals, and regional cuisine.

In conclusion, the best time to visit Sardinia depends on your interests. For beachgoers, the summer months offer the best conditions, while those seeking outdoor activities and cultural experiences might prefer the spring and early autumn. Traveling in the off-peak months can provide a quieter and more authentic experience, but be prepared for cooler weather in the winter. It's advisable to plan ahead and consider your preferences and priorities when deciding the ideal time for your Sardinian getaway.

2.2. ENTRY REQUIREMENTS AND VISA INFO

Sardinia, an enchanting island located in the Mediterranean Sea, is renowned for its stunning landscapes, rich history, and vibrant culture. If you're planning a visit to this Italian gem, it's essential to understand the entry requirements and visa information to ensure a smooth and enjoyable trip.

Entry Requirements:

As part of Italy, Sardinia follows the entry requirements set by the Schengen Agreement. Citizens of many countries, including the European Union member states and the United States, can enter Sardinia and stay for up to 90 days within a 180-day period for tourism, business, or family visits without requiring a visa. However, these travelers must possess a valid passport that remains valid for at least three months beyond their intended departure date.

For longer stays or other purposes such as work or study, different requirements might apply. It's recommended to check the specific entry regulations based on your nationality before traveling.

Visa Information:

1. Schengen Visa: Travelers from countries that are not part of the Schengen Agreement require a Schengen Visa to enter Sardinia. This visa allows entry into Sardinia and the entire Schengen Area for a short stay. The application process usually involves submitting a visa application to the Italian embassy or consulate in your home country, along with necessary documents such as a valid passport, proof of accommodation, travel itinerary, and travel insurance.

2. National Visas: If you plan to stay in Sardinia for an extended period, such as for work, study, or family reunification, you might need a national visa. This type of visa grants you the right to stay in Italy/Sardinia beyond the usual 90-day limit. The application process for a national visa is more complex and involves providing detailed information about your purpose of stay and additional documentation, such as letters of acceptance from educational institutions or job offers.

3. Residence Permits: For those planning to live in Sardinia for a more extended period, a residence permit is necessary. This is particularly applicable to non-EU citizens. The permit allows you to reside and potentially work/study in Sardinia for an extended duration. Application processes and requirements may vary depending on your circumstances.

It's important to note that visa requirements and regulations can change, so it's recommended to check with the official Italian consulate or embassy in your home country before planning your trip. Moreover, ensure you initiate the visa application process well in advance to allow for any potential delays.

In conclusion, Sardinia offers a captivating experience for travelers, and understanding the entry requirements and visa information is crucial to ensuring a seamless journey. Whether you're eligible for visa-free entry or need to apply for a Schengen Visa or national visa, make sure to have all the necessary documentation in order to fully enjoy the island's natural beauty, historical sites, and vibrant culture.

2.3. BUDGETING FOR YOUR TRIP

Budgeting for a trip to Sardinia involves careful planning to ensure you make the most of your experience without overspending. Here's a breakdown of essential aspects to consider while budgeting for your Sardinian adventure.

1. Flights and Accommodation:
Begin by researching flight and accommodation options. Prices may vary depending on the season and how early you book. Consider staying in

guesthouses or vacation rentals to save on lodging costs compared to upscale hotels.

2. Transportation:

Sardinia has a well-connected public transportation system, including buses and trains. If you plan to explore the island extensively, purchasing a transportation pass can be cost-effective. Alternatively, you can rent a car, which offers more flexibility but comes with fuel and parking expenses.

3. Meals and Dining:

Savoring Sardinian cuisine is a must. Opt for local trattorias and markets to experience authentic flavors at reasonable prices. Set a daily food budget and consider having a mix of restaurant meals and picnics to balance costs.

4. Activities and Sightseeing:

Do research about attractions and activities you want to experience. Some beaches and hiking trails are free, while others might have entrance fees. Prioritize the ones that align with your interests to avoid overspending on too many activities.

5. Souvenirs and Shopping:

Allocate a separate budget for souvenirs and shopping. Sardinia is known for its craftsmanship, including textiles, ceramics, and local wines. Plan ahead to avoid impulsive spending.

6. Miscellaneous Expenses:

Factor in unexpected expenses such as tips, minor medical costs, and internet charges. Having a buffer in your budget helps you stay prepared for any surprises.

7. Currency Exchange and Payment Methods:

Check the currency exchange rates and consider using a credit card with no foreign transaction fees. Notify your bank about your travel dates to prevent any payment issues.

8. Travel Insurance:

While it might seem like an additional cost, travel insurance can be a lifesaver in case of emergencies, flight cancellations, or medical issues. Factor this into your budget for peace of mind.

9. Flexibility in Spending:

Build some flexibility into your budget for spontaneous activities or opportunities that may arise during your trip.

10. Research and Pre-booking:

Advance research and booking can often lead to better deals on accommodations, transportation, and activities. Take advantage of discounts by booking ahead of time.

In conclusion, budgeting for your trip to Sardinia involves careful consideration of various expenses. By planning ahead, researching options, and allocating funds wisely, you can enjoy a memorable and affordable vacation on this beautiful Mediterranean island.

2.4. TRAVEL ESSENTIALS CHECKLIST

Preparing for your Sardinia adventure in 2023 involves careful planning and packing to ensure a smooth and enjoyable trip. A well-organized travel essentials checklist will help you cover all your bases and make the most of your journey to this stunning Italian island.

1. Travel Documents and Money:
Ensure you have your passport, travel insurance documents, driver's license (if needed), and any necessary visas. Don't forget to carry a copy of your passport in a separate location. Also, bring credit/debit cards and some local currency for convenience.

2. Clothing:

Sardinia's climate can vary, so pack a mix of lightweight clothing for the warm days and some layers for cooler evenings. Don't forget essentials like swimsuits, beach cover-ups, sun hats, and comfortable walking shoes for exploring.

3. Health and Personal Care:

Ensure to pack the medications you require, along with a basic first aid kit. Sunscreen, insect repellent, hand sanitizer, and any personal hygiene items should be on your list. If you plan to hike or be active, include blister pads and pain relievers.

4. Electronics:

Your phone, camera, chargers, and power adapters are crucial. A power bank can be a lifesaver during long days of sightseeing. Consider bringing a waterproof case for your devices, especially if water activities are on your agenda.

5. Outdoor Activities:

If you're planning on hiking, camping, or other outdoor activities, pack appropriate gear. Sturdy hiking shoes, lightweight backpacks, water bottles, and camping equipment might be necessary based on your plans.

6. Navigation and Language:

A detailed map of Sardinia or a GPS device can be immensely helpful for exploring. While many locals speak English, having a basic Italian phrasebook or translation app can enhance your experience and interactions.

7. Entertainment and Reading Material:

Long flights or downtime during your trip might warrant some entertainment. Pack books, e-readers, or download movies and shows onto your devices.

8. Snacks and Water:

Carrying some non-perishable snacks can be handy, especially if you're heading to remote areas. A reusable water bottle is eco-friendly and practical, considering the need to stay hydrated.

9. Weather Essentials:

Depending on the time of year, pack rain jackets, umbrellas, or light sweaters. Sardinia's weather can be unpredictable, so it's better to be prepared.

10. Beach and Water Activities:

Don't forget your beach towels, flip-flops, and snorkeling gear if you plan to explore the island's underwater beauty.

11. Reusable Bags:

A foldable tote bag or two can be incredibly useful for carrying souvenirs, groceries, or beach essentials.

12. Emergency Contacts and Important Numbers:

Have a list of emergency contacts, including local authorities, your country's embassy or consulate, and family members.

Remember that overpacking can be burdensome, so try to strike a balance between essentials and comfort. Tailor your checklist to your specific travel plans and preferences. With thorough planning and a comprehensive checklist, your Sardinia adventure in 2023 is bound to be an unforgettable experience.

2.5. GETTING TO AND AROUND SARDINIA

Sardinia, the second-largest island in the Mediterranean Sea, boasts stunning landscapes, rich history, and a unique culture. Getting to and around this Italian gem requires a combination of transportation modes that cater to both local charm and practicality.

Getting to Sardinia:

Most travelers reach Sardinia by air or sea. The island has three international airports: Cagliari-Elmas in the south, Olbia-Costa Smeralda in the northeast, and Alghero-Fertilia in the northwest. These airports offer flights from major European cities, making air travel a convenient option.

Ferries are also popular, especially for those traveling with vehicles. The main ferry ports are Cagliari, Olbia, Porto Torres, and Arbatax. Ferries connect Sardinia to mainland Italy and nearby islands, providing a scenic and relaxed mode of travel.

Getting Around Sardinia:

Sardinia's public transportation system includes buses and trains, though their coverage might not be as extensive as in some mainland regions. Buses are the primary mode of public transport, connecting major towns and cities. They offer a practical way to explore the island, with routes often extending to remote areas and tourist attractions.

For a more flexible travel experience, renting a car is highly recommended. This is particularly useful if you wish to explore Sardinia's hidden gems, picturesque coastal roads, and inland landscapes. However, driving can be challenging in some areas due to narrow roads and rugged terrain.

Local Transportation:

Within cities and towns, walking is a delightful option, allowing you to soak in the local atmosphere and admire historical architecture. Many urban areas also have reliable taxi services, which are especially handy during late hours or when public transport options are limited.

Cycling:

Sardinia's varied topography offers opportunities for cycling enthusiasts. Coastal roads, countryside routes, and mountain trails provide different levels of challenge for cyclists. Some areas have dedicated cycling lanes, and bike rentals are available in tourist hubs.

Boat Tours:

Since Sardinia is an island, boat tours are a fantastic way to explore its coastline and nearby islands. You can choose from guided tours or rent small boats for a more private experience. The crystal-clear waters and hidden coves make for unforgettable sailing adventures.

Language and Communication:

While Italian is the official language, Sardinian (or "Sardo") is still spoken by some locals and is recognized as a minority language. English might not be widely spoken in rural areas, so having a basic understanding of Italian phrases can be immensely helpful for communication.

In conclusion, Sardinia's unique blend of natural beauty, historical significance, and distinctive culture beckon travelers to explore its shores. Whether you choose to fly or ferry in, once on the island, a combination of buses, cars, and boats can help you navigate its diverse landscapes, from charming towns to serene beaches and rugged mountains. Remember to plan your transportation options based on your preferences and the areas you intend to explore.

2.6. HEALTH AND TRAVEL INSURANCE

Health and travel insurance play a vital role in ensuring a safe and stress-free experience for travelers visiting Sardinia, or any destination for that matter. Sardinia, known for its stunning landscapes, pristine beaches, and rich history, attracts a significant number of tourists each year. Having the right insurance coverage can offer peace of mind and financial protection in case of unexpected events.

Health insurance is crucial when traveling to Sardinia to ensure that you have access to medical care in case of illness or injury. While Sardinia has a well-developed healthcare system, visitors might not be eligible for free or low-cost medical treatment like residents.

Health insurance can cover medical expenses, hospitalization, prescription medications, and even medical evacuation if necessary. This is especially important considering that accidents or illnesses can occur at any time, and foreign medical costs can be exorbitant without proper coverage.

Travel insurance, on the other hand, offers a broader range of coverage. It not only includes health-related expenses but also addresses various travel-related issues. Trip cancellations or interruptions due to unforeseen events such as flight cancellations, natural disasters, or personal emergencies can be financially devastating. Travel insurance can provide reimbursement for nonrefundable expenses, ensuring that your investment in the trip is protected.

Moreover, travel insurance often includes coverage for lost or delayed baggage, travel document loss, and even liability coverage in case you cause accidental damage or injury to others during your trip. This comprehensive coverage can save you from unexpected expenses and complications that might otherwise turn your vacation into a nightmare.

When selecting health and travel insurance for Sardinia, or any destination, it's essential to carefully review policy details, coverage limits, and exclusions. Some insurance policies might have specific provisions related to adventure activities or pre-existing medical conditions, so it's crucial to choose a policy that aligns with your needs and travel plans.

In Sardinia, having health and travel insurance is a responsible and practical choice that can provide you with the support you need during unforeseen situations. Whether it's a sudden illness, a missed flight, or a lost suitcase, the right insurance coverage ensures that your travel experience remains enjoyable and worry-free.

Before embarking on your journey to Sardinia, take the time to research and select insurance plans that provide the appropriate level of coverage, allowing you to focus on creating cherished memories while exploring this captivating Italian island.

CHAPTER 3

ACCOMMODATION OPTIONS

3.1. HOTELS AND RESORTS

Sardinia, an enchanting island in the Mediterranean, is renowned for its stunning landscapes, turquoise waters, and rich cultural heritage. The island offers a variety of exquisite hotels and resorts that cater to travelers seeking both relaxation and adventure.

1. Costa Smeralda:
Located in the northeast of Sardinia, Costa Smeralda is known for its luxurious accommodations and pristine beaches. Hotels like Hotel Cala di Volpe, Hotel Romazzino, and Hotel Pitrizza offer upscale amenities and breathtaking views of the coastline. The region is also famous for its vibrant nightlife and exclusive boutiques.

2. Chia Laguna Resort:

Situated on the southern coast, Chia Laguna Resort boasts beautiful beaches and family-friendly accommodations. The resort includes multiple hotels such as Hotel Laguna, Hotel Baia, and Village. Guests can enjoy water sports, golf, and various activities for children.

3. Forte Village Resort:

Recognized as one of the world's best luxury family resorts, Forte Village is located in Santa Margherita di Pula. It offers a plethora of accommodations, including bungalows and villas. The resort features a wide range of dining options, sports facilities, and entertainment, making it ideal for both families and couples.

4. Hotel Capo d'Orso Thalasso & Spa:

Nestled in the north of the island, this hotel offers a tranquil escape with stunning views of the Maddalena Archipelago. Its private beach, spa, and exceptional service make it a popular choice for honeymooners and those seeking relaxation.

5. T Hotel:

Found in the heart of Cagliari, Sardinia's capital, T Hotel combines modern design with Sardinian charm. Its central location allows easy exploration of historic sites and vibrant city life.

6. Pullman Timi Ama Sardegna:

This family-friendly resort is set in Villasimius, offering direct access to a pristine beach. With spacious rooms, pools, and various activities, it's a great option for travelers seeking an active vacation.

7. L'Ea Bianca Luxury Resort:

Perched on the northern coast near Baja Sardinia, this elegant resort overlooks the crystal-clear waters of the Mediterranean. The boutique-style hotel offers a serene atmosphere, wellness facilities, and personalized services.

8. Su Gologone Experience Hotel:

Located inland near Oliena, this unique hotel showcases Sardinia's interior beauty. It features traditional decor, a renowned restaurant, and an art gallery displaying local crafts.

From the glamorous Costa Smeralda to the peaceful countryside retreats, Sardinia's hotels and resorts cater to a diverse range of preferences. Whether you're looking for a lavish beachfront experience or an authentic cultural escape, Sardinia offers a selection of accommodations that embody the island's natural beauty and warm hospitality.

3.2. BED AND BREAKFASTS

Bed and Breakfasts (B&Bs) in Sardinia offer a charming and unique accommodation experience that allows travelers to immerse themselves in the island's rich culture and stunning landscapes. Sardinia, known for its rugged coastline, crystal-clear waters, and vibrant history, provides an ideal backdrop for these cozy and personalized lodging options.

Sardinian B&Bs are often family-run establishments that provide a more intimate and authentic stay compared to traditional hotels. These accommodations range from quaint cottages and historic homes to modern villas, all of which showcase the island's distinctive architecture and design. Many B&Bs are situated in picturesque villages, offering visitors a chance to connect with local life and traditions.

One of the main draws of staying in a Sardinian B&B is the warm hospitality and personalized service offered by hosts. Travelers can expect a friendly welcome and insider tips on the best hidden gems, local attractions, and authentic dining experiences. This personal touch helps visitors gain a deeper understanding of Sardinian culture and enhances their overall travel experience.

Moreover, Sardinian B&Bs often provide home-cooked breakfasts featuring locally sourced ingredients, giving guests a taste of the island's culinary delights. The morning meal may include traditional Sardinian pastries, freshly picked fruits, and artisanal cheeses, showcasing the region's gastronomic heritage. This emphasis on local flavors also extends to the décor and ambiance of the accommodations, which often incorporate elements of Sardinian craftsmanship and design.

The island's diverse landscapes further enrich the B&B experience. From the rugged cliffs of the Costa Smeralda to the tranquil beaches of Chia, each B&B location offers a unique perspective on Sardinia's natural beauty. Some B&Bs even organize outdoor activities such as guided hikes, vineyard tours, and water sports, allowing guests to explore the island's wonders with the guidance of knowledgeable hosts.

While Sardinian B&Bs provide an intimate escape, they are also well-connected to the island's attractions. Many B&Bs are strategically located near historic sites, archaeological ruins, and cultural landmarks. This makes it convenient for guests to explore the island's past and present, whether wandering through ancient ruins or strolling along the bustling streets of Cagliari.

In conclusion, Bed and Breakfasts in Sardinia offer travelers a delightful blend of personalized hospitality, cultural immersion, and natural beauty. These charming accommodations provide a home away from home, allowing guests to experience the island's unique charm and character while enjoying the comforts of a cozy retreat. Whether seeking a romantic getaway or a family adventure, Sardinian B&Bs are an excellent choice for those looking to create lasting memories in one of Italy's most captivating destinations.

3.3. AGRITURISMOS AND RURAL STAYS

Agriturismos and rural stays in Sardinia offer an authentic and immersive experience for travelers seeking to connect with nature, local culture, and traditional ways of life. Nestled within the picturesque landscapes of Sardinia, these accommodations provide a unique opportunity to escape the hustle and bustle of urban areas and delve into the island's rural charm.

Sardinia, with its diverse geography ranging from rugged mountains to stunning coastlines, offers an ideal setting for agriturismos. These establishments are often family-run farms that have diversified their activities to include hospitality services. Visitors can expect warm hospitality, comfortable lodgings, and an introduction to the island's rich agricultural heritage.

Guests at agriturismos have the chance to participate in a variety of hands-on experiences, such as olive harvesting, grape picking, or cheese making, depending on the season. This interaction allows travelers to gain insight into traditional farming practices and local culinary traditions. Many agriturismos serve organic, locally sourced meals that highlight the flavors of Sardinian cuisine, often prepared using recipes passed down through generations.

The accommodations themselves range from charming rooms in renovated farmhouses to standalone cottages surrounded by vineyards or orchards. These lodgings typically blend rustic elements with modern comforts, providing an authentic yet comfortable stay. Guests can enjoy peaceful evenings under starlit skies, away from the noise of urban life.

Rural stays in Sardinia also offer opportunities for outdoor activities and exploration. Hiking trails, horseback riding, and guided tours allow visitors to appreciate the island's natural beauty, from the rugged interior to the pristine beaches. The charm of agriturismos lies in their ability to showcase the holistic experience of Sardinia, from its agricultural practices to its natural wonders.

Beyond the physical attractions, agriturismos contribute to the local economy and sustainable tourism. By supporting these establishments, travelers help maintain traditional livelihoods and preserve the rural landscapes that make Sardinia unique. Additionally, the interactions between guests and locals foster cultural exchange, as visitors gain a deeper understanding of Sardinia's history and way of life.

In conclusion, agriturismos and rural stays in Sardinia provide an enchanting opportunity for travelers to immerse themselves in the island's rustic beauty, vibrant traditions, and agricultural heritage. These accommodations offer an escape from the ordinary and a chance to experience the extraordinary aspects of Sardinian culture and landscapes.

Whether exploring the verdant countryside or indulging in locally sourced cuisine, visitors are sure to create lasting memories and connections during their stay in these idyllic settings.

3.4. COASTAL VILLAS AND RENTALS

Coastal Villas and Rentals in Sardinia offer an enchanting and luxurious escape for travelers seeking a unique blend of natural beauty, cultural richness, and leisure. Nestled along the stunning coastline of Sardinia, these villas provide an exclusive opportunity to indulge in the island's captivating charm while enjoying the comforts of a private, upscale accommodation.

Sardinia, the second-largest island in the Mediterranean, boasts a diverse landscape that ranges from pristine beaches with crystal-clear waters to rugged mountains and lush countryside. Coastal Villas and Rentals in Sardinia take full advantage of this picturesque setting, often offering panoramic views of the turquoise sea and golden beaches right from the property. This provides guests with an idyllic backdrop for relaxation and exploration.

These villas are meticulously designed to blend modern luxury with traditional Sardinian architecture. Many feature local materials like stone and wood, reflecting the island's unique cultural heritage. Spacious interiors, well-appointed kitchens, and upscale amenities ensure that guests experience a seamless combination of elegance and comfort. Private swimming pools, lush gardens, and outdoor lounging areas further enhance the experience, providing ample opportunities for leisure and entertainment.

One of the notable features of Coastal Villas and Rentals in Sardinia is their strategic locations. Many are situated within close proximity to charming villages, allowing guests to immerse themselves in the local culture and cuisine. Exploring traditional markets, sampling authentic Sardinian dishes, and engaging with the friendly locals add an enriching dimension to the stay.

Additionally, the coastal proximity grants easy access to a plethora of aquatic activities. Snorkeling, scuba diving, and boat excursions unveil the vibrant marine life that inhabits the surrounding waters. Guests can also explore hidden coves, sea caves, and remote beaches, discovering the untouched beauty that defines Sardinia's coastline.

The concept of Coastal Villas and Rentals in Sardinia extends beyond a mere stay; it's about crafting an unforgettable experience. Whether it's savoring a sunset dinner overlooking the sea, taking a leisurely stroll along the shore, or simply basking in the tranquility of the Mediterranean ambiance, these villas cater to a wide spectrum of preferences and desires.

In conclusion, Coastal Villas and Rentals in Sardinia offer a captivating fusion of luxury, natural splendor, and cultural immersion. With their breathtaking locations, opulent amenities, and proximity to both the sea and local life, these accommodations provide an exceptional opportunity for travelers to create cherished memories in one of the most alluring destinations in the Mediterranean.

3.5. UNIQUE ACCOMMODATION EXPERIENCES

Sardinia, the stunning Italian island in the Mediterranean, offers a plethora of unique accommodation experiences that go beyond the ordinary. From charming coastal villages to serene countryside landscapes, Sardinia provides an array of options for travelers seeking distinctive places to stay.

For those who crave an authentic maritime adventure, Sardinia's traditional fishing cabins, known as "casa campidanese," provide an immersive stay. These cabins, usually located near the shore, offer a direct connection to the island's seafaring heritage. Guests can enjoy the simple yet cozy interiors while relishing the tranquility of the sea.

For nature enthusiasts, the agriturismo accommodations are a perfect fit. These are farm stays that allow visitors to experience Sardinia's rural life firsthand. Guests can engage in farming activities, learn about local agriculture, and indulge in farm-fresh meals. The accommodations often retain their original rustic charm while incorporating modern comforts.

For a touch of luxury combined with nature, Sardinia offers unique glamping experiences. Imagine staying in a lavish tent or a treehouse amidst the island's picturesque landscapes. These accommodations blend the thrill of camping with the comfort of a hotel, providing an unforgettable stay under the starlit Sardinian sky.

Sardinia's historical towns also provide a glimpse into the island's rich past. Many historical buildings have been converted into boutique hotels, offering an opportunity to reside in centuries-old structures while enjoying contemporary amenities. These lodgings immerse guests in the island's history and culture.

Adventurous souls can explore the island's caves and cliffs by staying in a cave hotel. Carved into the rocky terrain, these unique accommodations provide a sense of seclusion while showcasing the geological wonders of Sardinia. It's an extraordinary way to connect with the island's geological heritage.

Sardinia's coastline, renowned for its turquoise waters, offers the chance to stay in stunning coastal retreats. Exclusive villas and beachside cottages provide direct access to the pristine beaches, allowing travelers to wake up to the soothing sounds of waves and bask in the sun's warmth just steps away from their doorstep.

In conclusion, Sardinia goes above and beyond in offering unique accommodation experiences that cater to a variety of tastes. Whether you're drawn to the historical charm of converted buildings, the rustic authenticity of farm stays, the glamor of glamping, or the maritime allure of fishing cabins, Sardinia has something for everyone.

These distinct lodgings not only provide a place to rest but also contribute to the overall adventure and memories of exploring this remarkable island in the Mediterranean.

CHAPTER 4

TRANSPORTATION AND NAVIGATION

4.1. PUBLIC TRANSIT AND BUSES

Public Transit and Buses in Sardinia: Connecting the Island Communities

Public transit and buses play a crucial role in the transportation infrastructure of Sardinia, an enchanting island nestled in the Mediterranean Sea. With its unique geographical characteristics and vibrant local culture, Sardinia relies on an efficient and comprehensive public transportation system to connect its diverse communities, facilitate tourism, and promote sustainable mobility.

Sardinia's public transit system primarily revolves around buses, which serve as the backbone of the island's transportation network. The bus routes cover both urban and rural areas, ensuring that even the most remote villages remain accessible. This connectivity is of paramount importance given the island's hilly terrain and scattered settlements.

The urban centers of Sardinia, such as Cagliari, Sassari, and Olbia, benefit from well-structured bus networks that enable residents to move around conveniently. These networks usually consist of regular routes within the city, catering to both local commuters and tourists. The buses are often equipped with modern amenities, making the travel experience comfortable.

In more rural regions, buses become a lifeline for residents who rely on them to reach essential services like healthcare, education, and shopping centers. These routes might have less frequent services due to lower population density, but they remain vital for maintaining community ties and ensuring equal access to resources.

Sardinia's tourism industry also greatly benefits from its public transit system. Tourists can explore the island's stunning landscapes, historic sites, and picturesque towns using the bus network. This helps alleviate traffic congestion and reduces the environmental impact of individual car rentals.

The regional government of Sardinia has been proactive in promoting sustainable mobility through its public transit initiatives. Investment in eco-friendly buses, incorporating renewable energy sources, and optimizing routes to minimize fuel consumption are some strategies employed to reduce the carbon footprint of the transportation system.

However, like any transportation network, Sardinia's public transit system faces challenges. Some remote areas might have limited or irregular bus services due to the logistical challenges posed by the island's topography. Additionally, ensuring the affordability of fares and maintaining the quality of services remains an ongoing effort.

In recent years, advancements in technology have played a role in enhancing Sardinia's public transit experience. Mobile apps provide real-time information about bus schedules, routes, and delays, empowering both residents and tourists to plan their journeys more effectively.

In conclusion, public transit and buses are integral to the fabric of daily life in Sardinia. They link the island's communities, enable sustainable tourism, and contribute to the overall well-being of its residents. As Sardinia continues to evolve, its public transportation system will likely play an increasingly important role in shaping the island's future by fostering connectivity, sustainability, and inclusivity.

4.2. CAR RENTALS AND DRIVING TIPS

Sardinia, with its stunning landscapes and picturesque coastlines, is a popular destination for travelers seeking a unique Mediterranean experience. When it comes to exploring the island, car rentals offer the flexibility and convenience to make the most of your trip. However, navigating Sardinia's roads requires some essential driving tips to ensure a safe and enjoyable journey.

Car rental options in Sardinia are abundant and can be found at major airports, cities, and tourist areas. It's advisable to book in advance, especially during peak travel seasons, to secure the best rates and vehicle availability. When choosing a car, consider the size of the vehicle based on the number of passengers and luggage. Opt for a vehicle that suits both your comfort and the type of terrain you plan to traverse. Keep in mind that many rental cars in Sardinia are manual transmission, so if you're more comfortable with automatic, be sure to request one ahead of time.

Driving in Sardinia offers an opportunity to explore the island at your own pace. However, it's essential to be aware of local driving rules and conditions. The roads in Sardinia vary from well-maintained highways to narrower coastal routes, often with winding turns. It's crucial to exercise caution, especially on rural roads, as they can be narrow and winding, requiring careful navigation. Speed limits are strictly enforced, so be sure to adhere to the posted limits, which are typically 50 km/h in urban areas, 90 km/h on rural roads, and 110-130 km/h on highways.

Navigation tools such as GPS or smartphone apps can be immensely helpful in Sardinia. They can guide you through intricate roads and lead you to breathtaking viewpoints and hidden gems. Cell phone coverage is generally reliable, but it's wise to download maps offline to ensure you don't lose access in remote areas.

Parking in Sardinia's towns and cities can be a bit challenging, especially in popular tourist spots. Blue lines on the curb often indicate paid parking zones, while white lines usually signify free parking areas.

As in any destination, it's important to be familiar with local traffic laws and customs. In Sardinia, seat belts are mandatory for all passengers, and driving under the influence of alcohol is strictly prohibited. Additionally, remember to carry your driver's license, rental agreement, and any necessary insurance documents.

In conclusion, car rentals provide an excellent way to explore the beauty of Sardinia. By following these driving tips and guidelines, you can make the most of your journey while ensuring a safe and enjoyable experience on the island's roads.

4.3. FERRIES AND ISLAND HOPPING

Ferries and Island Hopping in Sardinia:

Sardinia, the stunning Italian island in the Mediterranean, offers a unique experience for travelers through its extensive ferry network and the opportunity for captivating island hopping adventures. With its diverse landscapes, crystal-clear waters, and rich cultural heritage, Sardinia has become a prime destination for those seeking an unforgettable maritime journey.

Ferries serve as the lifeline connecting Sardinia's main island to its smaller counterparts. These vessels cater to both passengers and vehicles, facilitating convenient transportation between the islands. Major ferry ports such as Cagliari, Olbia, and Porto Torres provide gateways for travelers to embark on their island hopping quests. The ferry services are known for their reliability and efficiency, allowing tourists to seamlessly explore the various facets of Sardinia's beauty.

Island hopping in Sardinia presents an opportunity to delve into the island's distinct personalities. Maddalena Archipelago, a cluster of seven islands, is a popular starting point. Known for its white sandy beaches and turquoise waters, these islands offer a paradisiacal escape. The main island, La Maddalena, boasts charming villages and breathtaking viewpoints.

Moving north, Corsica emerges on the horizon as a feasible addition to the island hopping itinerary. With a mix of French and Italian influences, Corsica offers a blend of cultures, cuisines, and landscapes. The contrast between rugged mountains and pristine beaches is a testament to Corsica's diverse allure.

Continuing the journey, Asinara Island stands out with its unique history. Once a high-security prison, it has been transformed into a national park teeming with wildlife and untouched landscapes. Exploring the ruins of the former prison facilities while taking in the island's natural beauty creates an intriguing juxtaposition.

Culinary enthusiasts will find delight in island hopping as well. Each stop presents an opportunity to savor local delicacies and regional specialties. From Sardinia's own traditional dishes like "porceddu" (roast piglet) and "culurgiones" (stuffed pasta) to Corsican cheeses and wines, the gastronomic journey is as rich as the scenic one.

In conclusion, ferries and island hopping in Sardinia offer a comprehensive exploration of this remarkable region. The seamless ferry services ensure easy mobility between islands, while each destination provides a unique blend of history, culture, and nature.

From the captivating beaches of Maddalena Archipelago to the rugged charm of Corsica and the intriguing history of Asinara, Sardinia's islands beckon travelers to experience their captivating beauty and diverse offerings.

4.4. CYCLING ROUTES AND TOURS

Sardinia, the stunning Mediterranean island known for its diverse landscapes, rich history, and vibrant culture, offers cyclists a paradise of cycling routes and tours to explore its beauty. With its combination of coastal paths, mountain trails, and charming villages, Sardinia has become a sought-after destination for cyclists of all levels.

One of the most iconic cycling routes in Sardinia is the Costa Smeralda. This route takes cyclists along the breathtaking coastline, where azure waters meet rugged cliffs. The views are simply spectacular, making it an ideal option for those who enjoy both cycling and soaking in stunning panoramas.

For those seeking a more challenging adventure, the Gennargentu Mountains offer a series of demanding trails. These routes provide a glimpse into Sardinia's wild interior, with steep ascents and thrilling descents through dense forests and picturesque meadows. The reward at the top is often an unforgettable vista of the island's varied topography.

Sardinia's history and culture are deeply intertwined with its cycling routes. The Nuragic civilization, an ancient culture that inhabited the island, has left behind fascinating ruins that can be explored by bike. The Barumini Nuragic complex, a UNESCO World Heritage site, is easily accessible via cycling routes and offers a unique opportunity to combine physical activity with cultural enrichment.

Cycling tours in Sardinia are designed to cater to a wide range of preferences and abilities. Organized tours often include experienced guides who are familiar with the best routes, ensuring cyclists make the most of their journey. These tours can also provide insights into local traditions and cuisine, adding an immersive cultural dimension to the cycling experience.

In terms of logistics, Sardinia is cyclist-friendly. Bike rental shops are readily available in major towns and cities, offering a variety of bike types to suit different terrains. Many accommodations along popular cycling routes are equipped with facilities to store and maintain bikes, making it convenient for travelers to explore without worry.

Spring and autumn are generally considered the best seasons for cycling in Sardinia. The weather during these months is mild, allowing cyclists to enjoy their rides comfortably. It's essential to be prepared with proper gear, including helmets, hydration packs, and navigation tools, to ensure a safe and enjoyable journey.

In conclusion, Sardinia's cycling routes and tours offer an unforgettable blend of natural beauty, cultural exploration, and physical activity. Whether you're a leisure cyclist or a seasoned enthusiast, the island's diverse landscapes and well-designed routes promise an experience that's both invigorating and enriching. From coastal paths to mountain trails, Sardinia invites cyclists to discover its treasures on two wheels.

4.5. AIRPORT TRANSFERS

Airport transfers in Sardinia offer a convenient and efficient way for travelers to navigate between the island's airports and their desired destinations. Sardinia, known for its stunning beaches, historical sites, and vibrant culture, attracts a significant number of tourists each year. To cater to this influx, the region has developed a robust airport transfer infrastructure.

The primary airports in Sardinia are Cagliari-Elmas Airport, Olbia Costa Smeralda Airport, and Alghero-Fertilia Airport. These airports serve as the main entry points for visitors arriving from various parts of the world. Travelers have several options for airport transfers:

1. Shuttle Services: Many hotels and resorts in Sardinia provide shuttle services to and from the airports. These services are often pre-arranged and can be quite convenient for travelers looking for a hassle-free transfer. Shuttle services offer shared rides, making them a cost-effective choice.

2. Private Transfers: Private transfer services provide a more personalized experience. Travelers can book a private vehicle in advance, which is particularly beneficial for larger groups or families carrying extra luggage. The flexibility to choose the pick-up time and destination adds to the convenience of this option.

3. Taxis: Taxis are readily available at the airports and offer a convenient door-to-door service. However, they tend to be more expensive compared to shuttle or private transfer options.

4. Car Rentals: Renting a car is another popular choice for travelers who prefer to explore the island independently. Car rental companies have desks at the airports, allowing tourists to pick up their vehicles upon arrival. This option provides the freedom to travel at one's own pace and explore off-the-beaten-path destinations.

5. Public Transport: Public buses and trains also connect the airports to various parts of Sardinia. While this option is usually the most economical, it may not be the most convenient for travelers with a lot of luggage or those who are unfamiliar with the local transportation network.

When planning an airport transfer in Sardinia, it's advisable to consider factors such as the distance to your accommodation, the number of travelers, budget constraints, and personal preferences. Advanced booking of transfer services can help travelers secure their preferred mode of transportation and avoid last-minute hassles.

In conclusion, airport transfers in Sardinia play a crucial role in enhancing the travel experience for tourists arriving on the island. With a range of options available, travelers can choose the mode of transfer that aligns with their needs and preferences, ensuring a seamless journey from the airport to their chosen destination.

Whether it's a shared shuttle, a private transfer, a taxi, or a rented car, the variety of choices caters to the diverse requirements of visitors to this picturesque Mediterranean gem.

CHAPTER 5

SARDINIA'S NATURAL BEAUTY

5.1. BEACHES AND COASTLINES

Sardinia, an enchanting Italian island nestled in the Mediterranean Sea, boasts some of the most picturesque and captivating beaches and coastlines in the world. With its diverse landscapes, crystalline waters, and unique geological formations, Sardinia offers a haven for beach lovers and nature enthusiasts alike.

The island's coastline stretches for over 1,800 kilometers, revealing an assortment of stunning beaches that cater to various preferences. From secluded coves with hidden stretches of sand to expansive golden shores with vibrant local communities, Sardinia's coastal diversity ensures that every visitor finds their ideal spot. The Costa Smeralda, renowned for its upscale resorts and emerald-tinted waters, is a prime example of the island's luxury beach offerings.

What sets Sardinia's beaches apart is their incredible diversity. The west coast, facing the open sea, offers dramatic cliffs, rugged landscapes, and waves that attract surfers and water sports enthusiasts. In contrast, the east coast provides sheltered bays with calm waters, making it perfect for families and those seeking tranquility. The beaches in the south showcase white sands and shallow shores, making them an excellent destination for swimming and relaxation.

One of the island's most iconic landmarks is La Pelosa Beach in Stintino, renowned for its Caribbean-like setting with turquoise waters and fine white sands. The Spiaggia Rosa (Pink Beach) on the island of Budelli is another unique gem, featuring sand tinted with pink hues due to a mixture of crushed shells and coral fragments.

Sardinia's coastline isn't just about beaches; it also features striking geological formations. The Cala Luna, for instance, is accessible either by sea or by hiking through a scenic canyon. This beach is embraced by towering limestone cliffs that offer both shade and a dramatic backdrop. The Grotta di Nettuno (Neptune's Grotto) is a magnificent sea cave accessible from the sea or through a breathtaking stairway carved into the cliffside.

The local culture and history are intertwined with the beaches and coastlines of Sardinia. Many coastal towns showcase traditional architecture, colorful houses, and fishing communities that have thrived for generations. The island's cuisine, often centered around seafood, perfectly complements its coastal identity.

In conclusion, Sardinia's beaches and coastlines offer an unparalleled blend of natural beauty, cultural richness, and geological wonders. Whether you're seeking relaxation, adventure, or a glimpse into history, this island delivers a mesmerizing array of experiences. From hidden coves to bustling resort areas, Sardinia's coastal charm promises an unforgettable journey for every traveler.

5.2. NATIONAL PARKS AND RESERVES

Sardinia, the stunning Italian island in the Mediterranean, is renowned for its breathtaking landscapes, rich history, and unique biodiversity. The region boasts several national parks and reserves, each offering a distinct blend of natural beauty and cultural significance.

The Gennargentu National Park stands as one of Sardinia's most remarkable natural treasures. Encompassing the island's highest peaks and vast plateaus, the park is a haven for outdoor enthusiasts and nature lovers. Its rugged terrain and diverse ecosystems provide a habitat for a variety of plant and animal species, including the rare Sardinian deer and the golden eagle. Visitors can explore hiking trails that wind through ancient forests, encounter pristine lakes, and marvel at panoramic vistas that capture the essence of Sardinia's untamed spirit.

Asinara National Park, on the other hand, offers a unique contrast to the Gennargentu. This park is located on Asinara Island, just off the northwest coast of Sardinia. What was once a high-security prison has now been transformed into a sanctuary for diverse flora and fauna, many of which are endemic and rare. The park's marine area, a protected zone, houses flourishing seagrass meadows and underwater caves that support a wide array of marine life, making it a popular spot for snorkeling and diving enthusiasts.

Sardinia's national reserves, like the **Tavolara Punta Coda Cavallo Marine Protected Area**, emphasize the conservation of marine environments. This reserve spans the stretch of coastline from Tavolara Island to Punta Coda

Cavallo, encompassing vibrant coral reefs, seagrass beds, and important habitats for fish species. The reserve not only safeguards marine life but also promotes sustainable tourism and education about marine ecosystems.

The Monte Arcosu Nature Reserve is another remarkable site, celebrated for its efforts to protect the endangered Sardinian deer. The reserve's lush forests, rolling hills, and Mediterranean scrubland provide an ideal habitat for these deer, as well as other elusive creatures like the wild boar and the mouflon. Visitors can engage in guided tours that shed light on the reserve's conservation efforts and offer a chance to witness its remarkable biodiversity up close.

In conclusion, Sardinia's national parks and reserves are an integral part of the island's identity, preserving its unique landscapes and promoting ecological awareness. Whether it's the mountainous terrain of Gennargentu, the rehabilitated haven of

Asinara, the underwater wonders of marine reserves, or the conservation efforts at Monte Arcosu, each protected area contributes to the island's ecological health and cultural heritage.

These spaces not only serve as havens for biodiversity but also offer visitors a chance to immerse themselves in the natural wonders that make Sardinia an unparalleled destination for both adventure and appreciation of the natural world.

5.3. MOUNTAIN TREKS AND HIKING TRAILS

Sardinia, the second-largest island in the Mediterranean, offers a captivating blend of rugged landscapes, stunning coastline, and diverse terrain, making it a paradise for mountain treks and hiking enthusiasts. The island's topography ranges from high peaks to rolling hills, creating an array of trails suitable for various levels of hikers.

One of the most renowned mountain treks in Sardinia is the Gennargentu National Park, located in the heart of the island. The park boasts the highest peak in Sardinia, Punta La Marmora, which stands at an impressive 1,834 meters.

Hikers can explore challenging paths that wind through ancient forests, limestone plateaus, and rocky slopes. The Tacchi d'Ogliastra, unique rock formations resembling dolomite towers, present another intriguing hike. The Supramonte region, famous for its limestone gorges and caves, offers opportunities for adventurous trekkers to discover hidden natural wonders.

For those seeking coastal vistas, the Selvaggio Blu trail is a must. This challenging trek along the eastern coast combines breathtaking ocean views with rugged cliffs and dense Mediterranean vegetation. The trail spans around 50 kilometers and typically takes 6 to 7 days to complete, offering an immersive experience for seasoned hikers.

Less intense yet equally rewarding hikes can be found in areas like the Capo Testa Peninsula in northern Sardinia. Its easy-to-moderate trails guide hikers through dramatic rock formations, pristine beaches, and crystal-clear waters. The Monte Limbara range, located in the northern part of the island, offers a variety of paths suited for different fitness levels, surrounded by panoramic views of the surrounding valleys.

In southern Sardinia, the Sette Fratelli Mountains provide an ideal destination for those seeking shorter hikes. This protected area features well-marked trails that lead through Mediterranean scrubland, showcasing the island's diverse flora and fauna. Birdwatchers will find this region particularly appealing due to the variety of avian species present.

Sardinia's warm climate extends the hiking season throughout much of the year, with spring and fall being particularly popular times to explore the trails. To fully enjoy these treks, hikers are advised to come prepared with appropriate footwear, ample water, and a map or GPS device. It's important to respect the environment and local regulations while enjoying these natural wonders.

In conclusion, Sardinia's mountain treks and hiking trails offer a rich tapestry of natural beauty, ranging from towering peaks to coastal splendors. With trails catering to various skill levels and preferences, the island presents an enticing destination for adventurers seeking a unique blend of challenging terrain and breathtaking landscapes.

5.4. CAVES AND GROTTOES

Sardinia, an enchanting island in the Mediterranean, is renowned for its captivating natural landscapes, and among its remarkable features are its caves and grottoes. These geological wonders offer a glimpse into the island's ancient history, showcasing the intricate work of nature over millions of years.

The island boasts an array of caves and grottoes, each with its own unique characteristics. One of the most famous is the Grotta di Nettuno (Neptune's Grotto), situated on the Capo Caccia promontory near Alghero. Accessible by a dramatic stairway carved into the cliffs, this cave showcases stunning stalactite and stalagmite formations illuminated by the turquoise waters of the Mediterranean.

Another notable site is the Grotta del Bue Marino (Sea Ox Cave), located on the eastern coast of Sardinia. This expansive cave system, with its intricate chambers and underwater passages, was once inhabited by monk seals, giving rise to its name. It provides a glimpse into both geological wonders and the island's wildlife history.

The caves and grottoes of Sardinia also hold archaeological significance. The Grotta di Ispinigoli is home to one of Europe's tallest stalagmites, standing at around 38 feet. It has served as a natural time capsule, preserving evidence of prehistoric human presence, including ancient tools and artifacts.

One cannot discuss Sardinia's caves without mentioning the Grotte di Su Mannau, a network of underground chambers with impressive limestone formations. This site offers guided tours, providing visitors with a unique opportunity to explore its stunning speleothems, underground lakes, and narrow passages.

These caves and grottoes not only showcase the island's geological evolution but also its cultural and historical heritage. Their formations are a testament to the slow and patient work of nature, resulting in breathtaking landscapes that captivate visitors from around the world. Exploring these subterranean wonders is a journey through time, allowing us to connect with the deep-rooted history of Sardinia while being awe-inspired by the beauty that lies beneath its surface.

5.5. WILDLIFE WATCHING

Wildlife watching in Sardinia offers a unique and captivating experience for nature enthusiasts and travelers alike. Situated in the Mediterranean Sea, this Italian island boasts a diverse range of habitats, from rugged coastlines and lush forests to mountainous terrain, creating an ideal environment for observing a variety of wildlife species.

The island's coastline is a prime location for spotting marine life. Crystal-clear waters make it possible to witness the beauty of underwater ecosystems through activities like snorkeling and diving. In these waters, one can encounter an array of species, including colorful fish, dolphins, and even the elusive loggerhead sea turtle.

Moving inland, Sardinia's forests and mountains provide ample opportunities for birdwatching and observing terrestrial animals. The island is home to several species of raptors, such as the griffon vulture and Bonelli's eagle. Additionally, keen-eyed observers might spot the mouflon, a wild sheep species, as well as the rare Sardinian long-eared bat.

One of the most iconic and charismatic species that draws wildlife enthusiasts to Sardinia is the Sardinian deer. This native deer species can be found in the island's woodlands and open spaces. Its distinctive antlers and behavior make it a fascinating subject for observation and photography.

The Asinara National Park, located on an island just off Sardinia's northwest coast, is a particularly popular destination for wildlife watching. This protected area is home to a population of albino donkeys, along with other unique species. The park's isolation has allowed its ecosystem to remain relatively untouched, providing a haven for both native and reintroduced species.

To enhance the wildlife watching experience, Sardinia offers guided tours and nature excursions. Local experts and guides can lead visitors to the best viewing spots and provide insights into the behaviors and habitats of the island's wildlife. Whether on land or at sea, these knowledgeable guides contribute to a deeper understanding and appreciation of Sardinia's natural wonders.

In conclusion, wildlife watching in Sardinia offers an enchanting blend of marine and terrestrial experiences. From observing marine creatures in clear waters to spotting rare deer and captivating birds in diverse landscapes, the island provides a wealth of opportunities for nature enthusiasts to connect with the natural world. With its rich biodiversity and stunning scenery, Sardinia stands as a remarkable destination for those seeking an immersive wildlife watching adventure.

CHAPTER 6

CULTURE AND TRADITIONS

6.1. SARDINIAN CUISINE AND DELICACIES

Sardinian cuisine is a unique and rich culinary tradition hailing from the Italian island of Sardinia. It is characterized by its focus on simple, locally sourced ingredients, reflecting the island's agricultural heritage and rugged landscape. Sardinian cuisine has evolved over centuries, influenced by various cultures including Italian, Spanish, and North African, resulting in a diverse array of flavors and dishes.

1. Pane Carasau: This iconic Sardinian flatbread is paper-thin and crisp, often referred to as "music paper" due to its delicate layers. It's traditionally made using durum wheat flour and water, then baked twice to achieve its characteristic texture. Pane Carasau is commonly enjoyed with various toppings or dipped into soups.

2. Culurgiones: These handmade pasta dumplings are a staple of Sardinian cuisine. They are usually stuffed with a mixture of potato, mint, and cheese, then sealed into intricate shapes. Culurgiones are often served with a tomato or meat-based sauce, offering a burst of flavors and textures.

3. Porceddu: A beloved Sardinian dish, Porceddu is a whole roasted piglet seasoned with local herbs and cooked over an open flame or in a wood-fired oven. This dish is often the centerpiece of festive gatherings and celebrations.

4. Bottarga: A delicacy made from the salted and dried roe of gray mullet or tuna, Bottarga is commonly used as a seasoning. It's grated over pasta dishes like spaghetti or added to salads to provide a unique umami flavor.

5. Malloreddus: These small, ridged pasta shells are often referred to as Sardinia's version of gnocchi. They're typically served with a saffron-infused tomato sauce, creating a visually vibrant and aromatic dish.

6. Seadas: A delicious dessert that blends sweet and savory elements, Seadas consists of a thin pastry filled with a mixture of fresh cheese, lemon zest, and sometimes honey. The pastry is then deep-fried to a golden crispness and drizzled with honey.

7. Cannonau Wine: Sardinia is known for its robust red wine, Cannonau. Made from the Cannonau grape variety, this wine is rich and full-bodied, often boasting notes of dark fruit, spices, and a hint of smokiness. It's a perfect accompaniment to the island's hearty dishes.

8. Pecorino Sardo: This distinctive sheep's milk cheese comes in various forms, from soft and young to aged and crumbly. Pecorino Sardo is a versatile ingredient used in numerous Sardinian dishes, adding a rich, tangy flavor.

9. Fregola: Resembling small beads of pasta, Fregola is a type of semolina pasta that's toasted, giving it a nutty flavor. It's often used in soups and seafood dishes, absorbing flavors and providing a satisfying texture.

10. Sa Fregola con Arselle: This dish features Fregola pasta cooked with fresh clams and flavored with garlic, tomatoes, and parsley. It showcases the bounty of the sea and the skill of Sardinian chefs in combining simple ingredients to create complex flavors.

Sardinian cuisine embodies the island's history, geography, and cultural influences, resulting in a culinary experience that's both diverse and deeply rooted in tradition. From the hearty meat dishes to the intricate pastas and unique desserts, Sardinian cuisine offers a tantalizing journey through flavors and textures that reflect the island's vibrant heritage.

6.2. WINERIES AND WINE TASTING

Sardinia, the stunning Italian island in the Mediterranean, is not only renowned for its natural beauty but also for its flourishing winemaking tradition and exceptional wine tasting experiences. The island's unique terroir, a combination of climate, soil, and topography, plays a pivotal role in shaping the distinct characteristics of Sardinian wines.

Wineries in Sardinia boast a rich history, with some estates dating back centuries. The region's diverse microclimates provide an ideal environment for cultivating a variety of grape types, both indigenous and international. Vermentino, Cannonau, and Carignano are among the standout native grape varieties that thrive in Sardinia's vineyards. These grapes produce wines with distinct flavors and aromas reflective of the island's terroir.

Wine tasting in Sardinia is a captivating experience that often goes beyond the wine itself. Many wineries are nestled in picturesque landscapes, offering breathtaking views of the Mediterranean Sea or the island's rugged terrain. The ambiance and tranquility of the surroundings enhance the tasting journey, allowing visitors to immerse themselves in the culture and history of Sardinian winemaking.

Visitors to Sardinia can indulge in various types of wine tastings, ranging from casual samplings to guided tours. Guided tours typically take guests through the vineyards, explaining the viticulture practices that make Sardinian wines unique. Visitors learn about the winemaking process, from grape cultivation and harvesting to fermentation and aging. The tours often culminate in a tasting session, during which participants have the opportunity to savor a selection of wines produced on-site.

Sardinian wineries also often offer food pairings, allowing guests to experience the art of combining local cuisine with their wines. This enhances the tasting experience by showcasing how different flavors interact and complement each other.

Cannonau, a red wine made from the Grenache grape, is a flagship wine of Sardinia. Renowned for its potential health benefits due to its high levels of antioxidants, Cannonau exhibits rich flavors of dark fruits and a unique herbal undertone, which can be best appreciated during a guided tasting where experts explain its complexities.

In addition to Cannonau, Vermentino wines are another highlight. These white wines are crisp, refreshing, and often accompanied by floral and citrus notes. Carignano, a red grape variety, produces robust and full-bodied wines, reflecting the island's warmth and coastal influences.

In conclusion, Sardinia offers a captivating blend of history, tradition, and breathtaking landscapes within its wineries and wine tasting experiences. From its native grape varieties to the dedication of its winemakers, the island presents a unique opportunity for enthusiasts to explore and savor exceptional wines that capture the essence of this remarkable region.

6.3.   LOCAL   FESTIVALS   AND CELEBRATIONS

Sardinia, an enchanting island nestled in the heart of the Mediterranean Sea, boasts a rich tapestry of local festivals and celebrations that reflect its unique culture, history, and traditions. These events are a vibrant display of Sardinian identity and offer an opportunity for locals and visitors alike to immerse themselves in the island's authentic charm.

One of the most renowned festivals in Sardinia is "Sa Sartiglia," a colorful equestrian event celebrated in Oristano during the Carnival season. This centuries-old festival features masked horsemen demonstrating incredible skill as they attempt to pierce a star-shaped silver star with a sword while galloping through the town's narrow streets. The event is steeped in symbolism, representing the struggle between light and darkness.

Another significant celebration is "Sant'Efisio," held annually on May 1st in Cagliari. This religious procession is a testament to Sardinia's deep-rooted faith and cultural pride. Thousands of participants dressed in traditional attire accompany the statue of Saint Efisio on a 65-kilometer journey from Cagliari to the village of Nora. The procession passes through picturesque landscapes, and participants pay homage to the saint by wearing intricate costumes and showcasing Sardinian folk music and dance.

The "Autunno in Barbagia" festival, which takes place during the autumn months, provides a glimpse into Sardinia's rural life and artisanal traditions. Throughout various villages in the Barbagia region, visitors can explore workshops, taste local delicacies, and witness artisans practicing their time-honored crafts. From intricate handwoven textiles to exquisite pottery, this festival highlights the island's dedication to preserving its cultural heritage.

Sardinia's maritime heritage is celebrated during the "Cavalcata Sarda" festival in Sassari. Held on the third Sunday of May, this event showcases the island's connection to the sea. Colorful costumes, traditional music, and dancing accompany a procession that parades through the city streets, allowing locals and tourists alike to appreciate Sardinia's maritime roots.

Moreover, "Candelieri" is a remarkable event held in Sassari on August 14th. During this festival, enormous candlesticks are carried through the streets by groups of men, displaying immense strength and coordination. The candlesticks, which can weigh up to several hundred kilograms, are a testament to the town's history and are believed to bring protection and blessings.

In conclusion, Sardinia's local festivals and celebrations are a testament to its rich cultural heritage, providing an opportunity to delve into the island's unique traditions, rituals, and historical significance. These events not only celebrate Sardinia's religious and agricultural roots but also offer a chance for visitors to immerse themselves in the island's vibrant and lively atmosphere. Whether witnessing equestrian feats, religious processions, or artisanal showcases, attendees are sure to be captivated by the captivating spirit of Sardinia's local festivals.

6.4. CRAFTSMANSHIP AND ARTISANAL WORK

Craftsmanship and artisanal work hold a rich and culturally significant place in the beautiful island of Sardinia, known for its stunning landscapes and vibrant traditions. The island's artisans are renowned for their dedication to preserving age-old techniques and producing exquisite handmade goods that reflect the region's history and identity.

Sardinian craftsmanship is deeply rooted in the island's history, dating back to ancient times when skilled artisans crafted pottery, textiles, and intricate jewelry. These traditions have been passed down through generations, with artisans often learning their craft from family members or local masters. The commitment to preserving these techniques is a testament to the island's strong sense of cultural heritage.

One of the most notable aspects of Sardinian craftsmanship is its diversity. Each region of the island boasts its own specialized craft, resulting in a wide range of unique products. In the town of Samugheo, intricate handwoven textiles are produced using traditional looms. The village of Mamoiada is renowned for its wooden masks, which play a central role in the island's traditional carnival celebrations. Ceramists in the town of

Assemini create exquisite pottery adorned with intricate patterns, often inspired by the island's flora and fauna.

Artisans in Sardinia take great pride in using locally sourced materials, further enhancing the authenticity and sustainability of their creations. This commitment to traditional methods and materials ensures that each piece tells a story of the island's history and culture. Tourists and collectors are drawn to Sardinia to acquire these unique and meticulously crafted items, contributing to the local economy and supporting the continuation of these traditions.

The intricate process of crafting Sardinian artisanal products is a labor of love. Artisans invest hours of meticulous work into each piece, often using techniques that have remained unchanged for centuries. Whether it's hand-carving wooden statues, embroidering textiles, or hand-painting ceramics, the attention to detail and dedication to perfection are hallmarks of Sardinian craftsmanship.

While the modern world has brought changes to Sardinia, the island's artisans remain committed to their craft. Many workshops and studios are open to the public, allowing visitors to witness the creation process firsthand and appreciate the skill and passion that go into each piece. Additionally, cultural festivals and events showcase these artisanal works, serving as a platform to celebrate and promote Sardinia's rich heritage.

In conclusion, Sardinian craftsmanship and artisanal work are integral to the island's cultural fabric. The dedication to preserving traditional techniques, the use of local materials, and the diversity of crafts all contribute to the uniqueness of Sardinian artisanal products. These handmade creations not only reflect the island's history but also provide a glimpse into the soul of Sardinia itself.

6.5. FOLK MUSIC AND DANCE

Sardinia, the second-largest island in the Mediterranean, boasts a rich cultural heritage deeply intertwined with its distinctive folk music and dance traditions. The island's isolated geography has allowed these traditions to flourish over centuries, creating a unique tapestry of sounds and movements that reflect the island's history, society, and way of life.

Folk Music:
Sardinian folk music is characterized by its haunting melodies, intricate vocal harmonies, and the use of traditional instruments. One of the most iconic instruments in Sardinian music is the launeddas, a triple-piped reed instrument that produces mesmerizing and evocative tunes. This instrument, dating back to ancient times, is often associated with rituals and celebrations.

Another prominent Sardinian musical form is cantu a tenore, a style of polyphonic singing performed by a group of men. This captivating vocal technique involves four distinct voices creating harmonies that are both haunting and beautiful. The themes of the songs often revolve around pastoral life, love, and longing.

Folk Dance:

Sardinian folk dance is a vibrant and integral part of the island's cultural identity. Dances are often performed during festivals, weddings, and other communal events. One of the most famous Sardinian dances is the "Ballu Tundu," a circular dance where participants hold each other's hands and move in a graceful, rhythmic pattern. This dance reflects the island's strong sense of community and togetherness.

The "S'istrumpa," another traditional dance, is characterized by its lively footwork and intricate steps. Dancers often wear colorful costumes adorned with intricate embroideries that vary from region to region. These costumes not only add to the visual spectacle but also serve as a testament to Sardinia's diverse local cultures.

Cultural Significance:

Sardinian folk music and dance play a pivotal role in preserving the island's cultural heritage. The close connection between music, dance, and daily life showcases the importance of these art forms in the island's social fabric.

While modernization and globalization have inevitably impacted Sardinia, efforts are being made to ensure the survival of these traditions. Local festivals, workshops, and cultural organizations work tirelessly to promote and sustain folk music and dance, attracting both locals and tourists alike.

In conclusion, Sardinian folk music and dance embody the island's rich history and cultural diversity. The mesmerizing melodies, captivating harmonies, and graceful movements are a testament to the enduring spirit of a community deeply rooted in its heritage. As Sardinia continues to evolve, these traditions stand as a symbol of its identity and a bridge between its past and future.

CHAPTER 7

HISTORICAL SITES AND ARCHITECTURE

7.1. NURAGHE COMPLEXES

Nuraghe complexes are remarkable archaeological structures found on the Italian island of Sardinia. These ancient edifices are characterized by their unique stone construction and impressive architectural design, which has captivated historians and researchers for centuries.

Dating back to the Bronze Age, Nuraghe complexes are thought to have been built between the 18th and 9th centuries BCE. They are primarily composed of large, carefully stacked stone blocks, forming conical or cylindrical towers that can reach heights of up to 20 meters. The stone blocks were typically undressed, giving the structures a rugged and organic appearance. These complexes were likely used for defensive, religious, and social purposes within Sardinian society.

The main element of a Nuraghe complex is the central tower, which was surrounded by additional structures like courtyards, smaller towers, and sometimes even interconnected corridors. The purpose of these additional structures is still a subject of debate among researchers, with theories ranging from defensive fortifications to spaces for ritualistic activities or even residential areas. The interconnected corridors, if present, further highlight the advanced architectural knowledge of the Nuragic civilization.

The Nuraghe also exhibit intricate craftsmanship, evident in the meticulous construction and arrangement of stones. The complex designs, often laid without the use of mortar, showcase the technical prowess of the Nuragic people. Each Nuraghe complex was likely constructed over a considerable period of time, with additions and modifications made by successive generations, reflecting the evolving needs and aspirations of the society.

One of the most well-known Nuraghe complexes is Su Nuraxi di Barumini, a UNESCO World Heritage site since 1997. This site comprises a central tower surrounded by a defensive wall and smaller towers, providing a glimpse into the complexity of Nuragic architecture. The preservation of these structures offers valuable insights into Sardinia's past, shedding light on its prehistoric civilization's social structure, engineering capabilities, and way of life.

In conclusion, Nuraghe complexes are extraordinary remnants of Sardinia's ancient Nuragic civilization. Their distinct stone architecture, intricate designs, and multifunctional layouts continue to intrigue archaeologists and historians alike. These structures not only stand as testaments to the technical ingenuity of their creators but also provide valuable clues about the societal dynamics and cultural practices of Bronze Age Sardinia.

7.2. ANCIENT ROMAN RUINS

Ancient Roman ruins in Sardinia offer a captivating glimpse into the rich historical tapestry of the Mediterranean island. As a strategic outpost of the Roman Empire, Sardinia was home to various settlements and structures that have left behind enduring vestiges of their past.

The town of Nora, located on the southern coast of Sardinia, boasts an array of Roman ruins that speak to its historical significance. The Nora Archaeological Site features remnants of a well-preserved Roman theater, thermal baths, and intricate mosaics that showcase the opulence of the time. The city was founded in the 8th century BC by the Phoenicians and later became a Roman stronghold, eventually witnessing the cultural amalgamation of both civilizations.

Another prominent site is Tharros, situated on the west coast of the island. This ancient city was established in the 8th century BC by the Phoenicians and subsequently flourished under Roman rule. The ruins of Tharros reveal a Roman forum, temples, a residential quarter, and a necropolis. Notably, the Punic and Roman streets that meander through the site offer an authentic perspective on urban planning during that era.

Sardinia's Roman ruins also encompass the town of Cagliari, the island's capital. Here, the remains of an expansive Roman amphitheater provide insight into the grandeur of entertainment in ancient times. Additionally, the Roman Villa of Tigellio, an opulent villa showcasing exquisite mosaics and intricate frescoes, underscores the luxury enjoyed by the Roman elite.

Sardinia's historical significance as a crossroads of civilizations is further evident in its Roman aqueducts and engineering marvels. The Roman aqueducts of Sardinia, such as those found in the region of Sulcis, exemplify the empire's mastery over water management and distribution. These aqueducts facilitated the transportation of water across considerable distances, sustaining both urban centers and agricultural lands.

The enduring allure of Sardinia's Roman ruins lies not only in their architectural grandeur but also in their ability to transport modern visitors back in time. The interplay of Roman influence with the island's indigenous culture is palpable in the mosaic patterns, architectural styles, and inscriptions found among the ruins. As tourists explore these sites, they can't help but imagine the bustling life that once thrived within these ancient walls.

In conclusion, the ancient Roman ruins in Sardinia offer an immersive journey into the island's historical past. From the well-preserved theaters and temples to the intricate mosaics and aqueducts, these remnants showcase the indelible mark that Roman civilization left on this Mediterranean gem. The ruins not only bear witness to the empire's engineering prowess but also serve as a testament to the enduring allure of the past, inviting modern travelers to uncover the stories embedded within these stone remnants.

7.3. MEDIEVAL CASTLES AND FORTRESSES

Medieval castles and fortresses in Sardinia hold a significant place in the island's history, providing valuable insights into the region's architectural, cultural, and strategic evolution. Sardinia, located in the Mediterranean Sea, witnessed the construction of numerous castles and fortresses during the medieval period, each reflecting the various powers that ruled the island.

These structures served as defensive strongholds, safeguarding the inhabitants from external threats such as invasions by rival kingdoms, pirate raids, and marauding groups. The castles were typically built atop hills or rocky outcrops, maximizing their defensive potential and offering panoramic views of the surrounding landscape, allowing defenders to spot approaching danger from a distance.

One prominent example is the Castle of Acquafredda, also known as the Castle of Cagliari, which dates back to the 13th century. It played a crucial role in defending the city of Cagliari from attacks and stood as a symbol of authority during various ruling periods.

The Castle of Goceano, situated in the historical region of Logudoro, is another notable fortress. Constructed in the 12th century, it illustrates the strategic significance of castles in controlling key territories. It changed hands between various powers, including the Pisans, Aragonese, and Spanish, showcasing the island's historical complexities.

These castles and fortresses weren't merely military structures; they often evolved into thriving centers of administration, commerce, and culture. They housed royal residences, administrative offices, and places of worship. The Castle of Burgos in Alghero, constructed by the Catalan-Aragonese rulers, is an example of this multifunctional aspect. Its medieval architecture coexists with the Gothic-Catalan style, reflecting the diverse cultural influences present on the island.

Over time, with changing military technologies and geopolitical dynamics, the importance of castles as defensive structures diminished. As a result, many castles fell into disrepair and were abandoned. However, in recent decades, efforts have been made to preserve and restore these historical sites. They attract tourists and researchers alike, offering a glimpse into Sardinia's medieval past and its connections to wider Mediterranean history.

In conclusion, medieval castles and fortresses in Sardinia serve as tangible remnants of the island's intricate history. They embody the struggles, triumphs, and cultural interactions that shaped Sardinia's identity. From their strategic positioning to their architectural features, these structures offer a window into the past and continue to captivate the imagination of those who explore them.

7.4. PHOENICIAN AND CARTHAGINIAN SITES

Sardinia, an island located in the Mediterranean Sea, boasts a rich historical heritage intertwined with the Phoenician and Carthaginian civilizations. These ancient maritime powers left behind a legacy of significant archaeological sites that provide insights into their cultural, economic, and political influence on the island.

Phoenician settlements on Sardinia date back to the 9th century BCE, as these seafaring traders established trading posts along the coastline. Notable Phoenician sites include Nora, Tharros, and Bithia. Nora, located on the southern tip of the island, features well-preserved ruins of a Phoenician settlement that eventually became a Carthaginian and Roman city. The site includes remnants of temples, houses, and a unique Punic-Roman theater.

Tharros, situated on the west coast, is another important Phoenician-Carthaginian archaeological site. Its strategic location made it a thriving port and trading hub during ancient times. The site showcases ruins of fortifications, a tophet (sacred precinct), and Roman baths, reflecting the layers of cultures that inhabited the area.

Bithia, near Chia, provides evidence of early Phoenician colonization. This site offers a glimpse into the island's maritime history through its ancient shipyard and tophet. These Phoenician settlements gradually came under Carthaginian control as Carthage grew in power, leading to the establishment of Carthaginian dominance on the island.

Carthage, a powerful city-state in North Africa, extended its influence over Sardinia in the 6th century BCE. The Carthaginians constructed fortified towns and strongholds across the island to solidify their control and protect their interests. The city of Karales (modern-day Cagliari) became a key Carthaginian center, boasting defensive walls, temples, and other structures that reflected the city's significance as an administrative and military hub.

One of the most striking Carthaginian sites is Monte Sirai, a hilltop settlement showcasing a fusion of Phoenician and Carthaginian architectural elements. This site provides valuable insights into the Carthaginian way of life, including religious practices and urban planning.

In conclusion, the Phoenician and Carthaginian sites in Sardinia stand as a testament to the island's historical importance as a crossroads of ancient civilizations. These sites offer a window into the economic, cultural, and political dynamics that shaped the region. The remnants of temples, fortifications, theaters, and other structures highlight the enduring impact of these civilizations on Sardinia's history and heritage. Exploring these sites allows us to unravel the complex tapestry of the Phoenician and Carthaginian presence in the Mediterranean and their lasting influence on this enchanting island.

7.5. ARCHAEOLOGICAL MUSEUMS

Archaeological museums in Sardinia offer a captivating glimpse into the island's rich and diverse history, showcasing its ancient civilizations, cultures, and artifacts. These museums serve as repositories of Sardinia's past, shedding light on its prehistoric, Nuragic, Roman, and medieval periods.

The National Archaeological Museum of Cagliari, located in the island's capital, stands as one of the most prominent institutions of its kind. Its exhibits span several millennia, featuring a remarkable collection of Nuragic bronzes, Phoenician ceramics, and Roman artifacts. The museum provides an immersive experience, allowing visitors to trace the evolution of Sardinia's societies through its extensive displays.

Tharros Archaeological Museum, situated on the western coast, is another highlight. It focuses on the ancient city of Tharros and its surroundings, offering insights into the Phoenician, Punic, and Roman periods. The museum's displays include sculptures, pottery, and intricate mosaics, providing a vivid picture of daily life and cultural exchanges in antiquity.

The Museo Archeologico Nazionale di Olbia, located in the north, showcases the maritime heritage of Sardinia. Olbia's strategic position in the

Mediterranean made it a hub for trade and cultural interactions. The museum exhibits artifacts recovered from underwater archaeological sites, offering a unique perspective on Sardinia's interconnected past.

One cannot discuss Sardinian archaeology without mentioning the Nuragic civilization, which flourished on the island from the Bronze Age to the Roman conquest. The Museo Nazionale Archeologico ed Etnografico G.A. Sanna in Sassari delves into this civilization, displaying Nuragic artifacts including intricate bronze statuettes, ceramic vessels, and architectural models of Nuraghe complexes.

The archaeological museums in Sardinia not only showcase physical artifacts but also contribute to ongoing research and educational efforts. They provide platforms for scholars, archaeologists, and historians to collaborate and share their findings, contributing to a deeper understanding of the island's past.

Visiting these museums is akin to embarking on a time-traveling journey. The artifacts on display offer windows into Sardinia's history, allowing visitors to connect with the island's ancient inhabitants and their way of life. The curatorial efforts and presentation techniques in these museums ensure that the historical narrative is accessible and engaging to a wide range of audiences, from scholars to tourists.

In conclusion, Sardinia's archaeological museums play a vital role in preserving, studying, and sharing the island's rich history. Through their exhibits, they illuminate the multifaceted tapestry of civilizations that have shaped Sardinia over millennia, leaving an indelible mark on its culture and identity.

CHAPTER 8

WATER SPORTS AND RECREATION

8.1. SCUBA DIVING AND SNORKELING

Sardinia, with its crystal-clear waters and stunning coastline, offers an idyllic setting for both scuba diving and snorkeling enthusiasts. These water-based activities provide unique opportunities to explore the rich marine life, vibrant coral reefs, and underwater caves that characterize the island's aquatic ecosystem.

Scuba diving in Sardinia is a mesmerizing adventure that attracts divers from around the world. The island boasts a diverse range of dive sites suitable for both beginners and experienced divers. The La Maddalena Archipelago, a protected marine area, is renowned for its underwater biodiversity. Divers can encounter an array of marine species, including colorful fish, octopuses, and even dolphins. The Posidonia seagrass meadows in Sardinia's waters play a crucial role in maintaining the health of the marine environment, making for unique diving experiences.

One of the most sought-after diving locations in Sardinia is the Neptune's Grotto cave. Located on the breathtaking Capo Caccia cliff, this underwater cave showcases stunning stalactites and stalagmites. The Grotto is accessible through guided tours and offers an otherworldly experience for divers to explore its hidden chambers and corridors.

For those seeking a more accessible and leisurely underwater experience, snorkeling in Sardinia is equally enchanting. The calm and shallow waters along the coast make snorkeling an ideal option for individuals of all ages. Exploring the vibrant Mediterranean underwater world becomes an immersive activity as snorkelers glide above colorful marine life and coral formations.

Cala Mariolu, a pristine cove known for its azure waters and white pebble beach, is a snorkeler's paradise. The bay's clear waters provide excellent visibility, allowing snorkelers to observe a kaleidoscope of fish species and marine flora. Another gem is Tuerredda Beach, where snorkelers can discover the underwater wonders of Posidonia meadows and perhaps spot small rays or seahorses.

Both scuba diving and snorkeling experiences in Sardinia benefit from the island's commitment to marine conservation. Local operators and dive centers emphasize responsible diving practices, ensuring minimal impact on the delicate marine ecosystems. As a result, divers and snorkelers not only enjoy the beauty of Sardinia's underwater world but also contribute to its preservation.

In conclusion, Sardinia's inviting waters beckon both scuba divers and snorkelers to explore the diverse marine life and stunning landscapes beneath the surface. With a plethora of dive sites, from intricate caves to vibrant reefs, the island offers unforgettable experiences for water enthusiasts of all skill levels. Whether choosing the depths of scuba diving or the tranquility of snorkeling, Sardinia's aquatic wonders are bound to leave an indelible impression.

8.2. SAILING AND YACHTING

Sailing and yachting in Sardinia offer an unparalleled experience for enthusiasts and travelers alike. Situated in the heart of the Mediterranean, Sardinia boasts stunning coastlines, crystal-clear waters, and a rich maritime heritage that makes it a prime destination for sailing and yachting activities.

With its favorable climate, steady winds, and diverse landscapes, Sardinia provides ideal conditions for both beginners and experienced sailors. The island's numerous ports, marinas, and anchorages cater to various needs, ensuring a comfortable and accessible sailing experience. From the glamorous Costa Smeralda to the more tranquil Gulf of Orosei, the island offers a wide range of sailing routes that allow visitors to explore its natural beauty and cultural richness.

One of the most renowned locations for sailing and yachting in Sardinia is the Costa Smeralda. This exclusive stretch of coastline is famous for its luxurious resorts, upscale marinas, and vibrant nightlife. It has become a playground for the rich and famous, attracting high-end yachts from around the world. The Maddalena Archipelago, located nearby, provides an exquisite backdrop for cruising, with its emerald waters and secluded coves.

For those seeking a more serene sailing experience, the Gulf of Orosei on the eastern coast of Sardinia offers breathtaking landscapes, including towering limestone cliffs, hidden caves, and pristine beaches accessible only by boat. Exploring this area by yacht allows travelers to access remote spots that remain untouched by mass tourism.

Sardinia's maritime culture and history are deeply ingrained in its identity. The island has a long tradition of seafaring, fishing, and boat craftsmanship. Visitors have the opportunity to immerse themselves in this heritage by participating in local regattas, interacting with fishermen, or even trying their hand at traditional boat building.

It's important to note that the preservation of the marine environment is of utmost importance in Sardinia. Sustainable sailing practices are encouraged to protect the delicate ecosystems and maintain the beauty that draws people to the island. Many local organizations and authorities collaborate to promote responsible yachting and eco-friendly tourism.

In conclusion, Sardinia's allure for sailing and yachting enthusiasts lies in its combination of stunning natural beauty, diverse sailing routes, and rich cultural heritage. Whether you're looking for a glamorous yachting experience along the Costa Smeralda or a peaceful journey through the Gulf of Orosei's hidden gems, Sardinia offers a sailing adventure that is both unforgettable and deeply rewarding.

8.3. WINDSURFING AND KITEBOARDING

Windsurfing and kiteboarding are two exhilarating water sports that have gained immense popularity in the stunning island of Sardinia, Italy. With its crystal-clear waters, consistent winds, and breathtaking landscapes, Sardinia offers the perfect playground for enthusiasts of these adrenaline-pumping activities.

Windsurfing, a dynamic sport that combines elements of both sailing and surfing, involves riding a board while holding onto a sail attached to a mast. The wind propels the board forward, allowing the surfer to perform impressive maneuvers and tricks. Sardinia's diverse coastline provides a range of conditions suitable for windsurfing, from gentle bays for beginners to challenging waves and strong winds for advanced riders. Locations like Porto Pollo and Costa Smeralda are particularly renowned among windsurfers due to their reliable wind patterns and top-notch facilities. The Mistral and Scirocco winds that sweep across the island ensure a thrilling experience for windsurfing aficionados.

Kiteboarding, also known as kitesurfing, is another thrilling water sport that has captured the hearts of adventure seekers in Sardinia. Participants strap their feet onto a board and harness themselves to a large controllable kite. By manipulating the kite's movements, kiteboarders can soar through the air and perform gravity-defying tricks above the waves. Sardinia's flat and shallow waters, especially in spots like Porto Botte and Punta Trettu, make it an ideal destination for kiteboarding. The constant winds and ample space ensure an unforgettable experience for both beginners and experienced riders.

Sardinia's geography provides a diverse range of conditions for windsurfing and kiteboarding. The northern coast with its granite cliffs and sandy beaches offers a mix of calm waters and stronger winds, while the southern coast boasts long stretches of sandy shores and gentle breezes. The island's consistent winds are attributed to its geographical position in the Mediterranean, making it a year-round destination for these sports.

Both windsurfing and kiteboarding in Sardinia are supported by a robust infrastructure of rental shops, schools, and specialized centers offering lessons for all skill levels. Whether you're a complete novice or a seasoned pro, there's an opportunity to learn, improve, and enjoy these sports in the picturesque surroundings of Sardinia.

In conclusion, Sardinia stands out as a premier destination for windsurfing and kiteboarding due to its stunning natural beauty, favorable wind conditions, and well-developed water sports infrastructure. Enthusiasts of these sports are treated to an unforgettable experience as they glide over the azure waters, surrounded by the breathtaking landscapes that only Sardinia can offer.

8.4. KAYAKING AND CANYONING

Sardinia, with its rugged coastline and diverse landscapes, offers outdoor enthusiasts an ideal setting for both kayaking and canyoning adventures. These thrilling activities allow visitors to explore the island's natural beauty from unique perspectives, immersing themselves in its stunning waters and hidden gorges.

Kayaking in Sardinia presents an opportunity to navigate along its picturesque coastline, which boasts turquoise waters and dramatic cliffs. Novices can opt for guided tours in calm waters, while seasoned kayakers can challenge themselves by exploring sea caves and remote beaches. The

Maddalena Archipelago, located off the northeastern coast, is a popular destination for kayakers, offering crystal-clear waters and secluded coves.

Additionally, the Gulf of Orosei on the eastern coast is renowned for its limestone cliffs and hidden sea caves that can be explored by kayak. The sport allows for a serene connection with nature, granting glimpses of marine life and breathtaking coastal vistas.

Canyoning, on the other hand, offers a more inland adventure, allowing participants to explore the island's rugged interior. Sardinia's mountainous terrain is adorned with gorges, waterfalls, and canyons that beckon adventurers. The Rio Pitrisconi Canyon is a prominent canyoning destination, known for its thrilling descents, natural water slides, and refreshing pools.

Another notable site is the Gola di Gorroppu, one of Europe's deepest canyons. Canyoning here involves rappelling down waterfalls and traversing narrow passages, surrounded by steep rock walls. The sport offers a unique blend of adrenaline-pumping activities and awe-inspiring natural beauty.

Both kayaking and canyoning in Sardinia are often facilitated by experienced guides who prioritize safety while ensuring a memorable experience. They provide necessary equipment, guidance, and insights into the local geography and ecosystems. These activities also offer a chance to learn about Sardinia's rich cultural history, as the landscapes often hold archaeological sites and remnants of ancient civilizations.

In conclusion, kayaking and canyoning in Sardinia offer adventurers an extraordinary opportunity to explore the island's diverse landscapes. Whether gliding through tranquil waters along the coast or descending into stunning canyons in the heart of the island, these activities provide an immersive way to appreciate Sardinia's natural wonders. With its captivating mix of Mediterranean beauty and thrilling challenges, Sardinia stands out as an exceptional destination for outdoor enthusiasts seeking unforgettable experiences.

8.5. FISHING AND BOAT TOURS

Sardinia, an enchanting Mediterranean island, offers a unique blend of stunning natural beauty and rich cultural experiences, attracting travelers from around the globe. Among its many attractions, fishing and boat tours stand out as exceptional ways to explore the island's coastal splendor and engage with its maritime traditions.

Fishing in Sardinia is not merely an activity; it's a way of life that has been passed down through generations. The island's crystal-clear waters teem with an abundance of marine life, making it a paradise for fishing enthusiasts. From amateur anglers to seasoned pros, there's something for everyone. The variety of fish available includes red mullet, sea bream, and tuna, making for exciting and rewarding catches. Local fishing charters and guides offer opportunities for both deep-sea fishing and inshore angling, allowing visitors to experience the thrill of reeling in impressive catches while soaking in the stunning coastal views.

For those seeking a more leisurely maritime experience, boat tours around Sardinia's coastline are an absolute must. The island boasts a diverse range of boat tours, each offering a unique perspective on its natural wonders. From serene sunset cruises to adventurous snorkeling expeditions, there's a tour suited for every taste. One can explore the mesmerizing sea caves, such as the famous Grotta di Nettuno (Neptune's Grotto), with their intricate formations and captivating hues. Additionally, boat tours provide a vantage point to witness the island's dramatic cliffs, hidden coves, and pristine beaches that are otherwise inaccessible.

These tours often weave in the island's rich cultural history. Sardinia's maritime heritage is showcased as guides share stories of ancient seafaring traditions, which were integral to the island's survival and prosperity. Visitors can gain insights into the art of traditional fishing techniques, like the "tonnara" (tuna fishing) that was practiced for centuries. The island's fishing villages, such as Alghero and Calasetta, further immerse tourists in its coastal culture, offering delectable seafood cuisines and vibrant markets brimming with local crafts and products.

In conclusion, fishing and boat tours in Sardinia offer an enchanting blend of nature, culture, and adventure. The island's thriving marine life and awe-inspiring coastal landscapes make it a prime destination for fishing enthusiasts and those seeking maritime explorations.

Whether one chooses to cast a line into the deep blue waters or embark on a boat tour to uncover hidden gems along the coastline, Sardinia promises an unforgettable experience that celebrates its rich maritime heritage and the beauty of the Mediterranean.

CHAPTER 9

LOCAL CUISINE AND DINING

9.1. SARDINIAN CULINARY TRADITIONS

Sardinian culinary traditions are deeply rooted in the island's history, geography, and cultural heritage. Situated in the Mediterranean Sea, Sardinia's cuisine is a reflection of its diverse influences, blending elements from Italy, Spain, North Africa, and even the Middle East. The island's isolation has played a significant role in shaping its unique culinary identity.

One of the defining features of Sardinian cuisine is its emphasis on locally sourced and seasonal ingredients. The island's rugged terrain and agricultural practices have given rise to dishes that prominently feature ingredients like sheep's milk, grains, legumes, and wild herbs. Pecorino cheese, made from sheep's milk, is a staple in Sardinian households and features prominently in many traditional dishes.

One of the most iconic dishes of Sardinia is "porceddu," a roasted suckling pig. Prepared by marinating the pig with local herbs and spices before slow-roasting it, porceddu results in tender meat with a crispy, flavorful skin. Another notable dish is "malloreddus," a type of pasta that is often served with a saffron-infused tomato sauce or a meat ragù. This dish showcases the island's use of indigenous saffron, which adds both color and flavor to many recipes.

Seafood plays a significant role in Sardinian cuisine due to the island's proximity to the Mediterranean Sea. Dishes like "fregola con arselle" (a type of pasta with clams) and "bottarga" (salted, cured fish roe) highlight the island's coastal culinary offerings. "Zuppa gallurese" is a hearty bread and cheese casserole that is layered with flavorful broth, showcasing the creative use of simple ingredients.

Sardinians have also perfected the art of preserving food, likely influenced by the island's historical isolation. "Pane carasau," a paper-thin, crisp bread, can last for months and was traditionally carried by shepherds during their journeys. It's often enjoyed with olive oil, tomatoes, and various toppings. Another example is "culurgiones," a type of stuffed pasta typically filled with a mixture of potatoes, cheese, and mint, showcasing Sardinia's knack for creating satisfying, long-lasting dishes.

The island's beverages are equally noteworthy. Sardinia boasts unique wines, such as the full-bodied red Cannonau, which is believed by some to contribute to the island's high rate of centenarians. "Filu 'e ferru" or "thread of iron" is a traditional Sardinian moonshine with historical roots in resistance to taxation during Italian unification.

In conclusion, Sardinian culinary traditions are a testament to the island's rich history, geographical isolation, and cultural diversity. From hearty meat dishes and aromatic pastas to artisanal cheeses and distinctive wines, Sardinia's cuisine is a vibrant tapestry woven with local ingredients and a strong sense of identity.

9.2. SEAFOOD RESTAURANTS

Sardinia, the stunning Italian island nestled in the Mediterranean, boasts a rich culinary scene renowned for its seafood delicacies. Here, seafood restaurants flourish, offering a tantalizing array of dishes that celebrate the bounties of the surrounding waters. Let's delve into some of the prominent seafood restaurants in Sardinia:

1. Ristorante Da Giovanni: Located in the charming coastal town of Alghero, this restaurant is famed for its traditional Sardinian seafood cuisine. With a focus on fresh catch, the menu showcases dishes like bottarga (cured fish roe), fregola con arselle (a clam and semolina pasta), and grilled octopus. The rustic ambiance and seaside views add to the dining experience.

2. Sa Cardiga e Su Pisci: Nestled in a quaint village, this establishment offers an authentic taste of Sardinian seafood. The menu highlights a variety of seafood stews, where the catch of the day is simmered with tomatoes, onions, and aromatic herbs. The restaurant's commitment to traditional recipes sets it apart.

3. La Pelosa Beach: This beachfront gem in Stintino not only provides pristine white sands and crystal-clear waters but also features beachside seafood dining. Imagine relishing grilled fish, fresh seafood salads, and local wines while gazing at the mesmerizing sunset over the Gulf of Asinara.

4. Trattoria Da Angelo: Situated in Cagliari, the island's capital, this trattoria combines seafood with a contemporary twist. Alongside classic dishes like spaghetti alle vongole (clam pasta), you'll find innovative creations such as sea urchin risotto, showcasing the fusion of traditional flavors and modern techniques.

5. Su Gologone: While not directly on the coast, this restaurant near the Supramonte Mountains is renowned for its seafood specialties. Freshness is paramount here, with ingredients sourced from both land and sea. The menu features an array of seafood antipasti, culminating in unforgettable seafood platters.

6. Ristorante La Spigola: Overlooking the Gulf of Arzachena, this restaurant in Costa Smeralda offers a refined dining experience. La Spigola is synonymous with fish, as its name translates to "sea bass." Enjoy expertly prepared fish dishes like grilled sea bass and fish carpaccio in an elegant setting.

7. Ristorante Belvedere: Found in Palau, this restaurant capitalizes on its scenic location, affording panoramic views of the Maddalena Archipelago. Specializing in seafood, it offers a wide array of dishes ranging from the catch of the day to more elaborate seafood platters, all served with a touch of Mediterranean flair.

8. Ristorante Stella Marina: Perched along the Gulf of Orosei, this restaurant combines its breathtaking coastal location with a seafood-centric menu. Indulge in dishes like lobster linguine and seafood risotto while being serenaded by the gentle sound of the waves.

In Sardinia, seafood restaurants are more than just places to dine; they encapsulate the island's maritime culture and culinary heritage. From rustic trattorias to upscale establishments, these eateries offer an unparalleled opportunity to savor the treasures of the sea while basking in the island's natural beauty. Each restaurant mentioned above contributes to the mosaic of flavors that make

Sardinia's seafood scene a gastronomic treasure trove.

9.3. TRADITIONAL SARDINIAN DISHES

Sardinia, an island located in the Mediterranean Sea, boasts a rich culinary tradition that reflects its diverse history, geographical location, and local ingredients. Traditional Sardinian dishes are characterized by their simplicity, reliance on locally sourced ingredients, and deep-rooted cultural significance.

One iconic dish is "Porceddu," a roasted suckling pig prepared with aromatic herbs and cooked on a spit. This dish is often the centerpiece of celebratory gatherings and showcases the island's agricultural heritage. Another culinary delight is "Culurgiones," a type of filled pasta. These dumplings are typically stuffed with a mixture of potatoes, pecorino cheese, and mint, and their intricate shape reflects the island's artistic flair.

Sardinian cuisine is also renowned for its use of staple ingredients like "Pane Carasau," a crispy flatbread that was historically favored by shepherds due to its long shelf life. It's often enjoyed with local cheeses, olives, and cured meats. Speaking of cheeses, "Pecorino Sardo" is a standout. Made from sheep's milk, this cheese comes in various aging stages, each with a distinct flavor profile.

Seafood plays a significant role in Sardinian gastronomy due to its coastal location. "Fregola con Arselle" is a dish featuring small balls of semolina pasta cooked with clams and a flavorful tomato-based broth. "Bottarga," a delicacy made from dried fish roe, is grated over pasta dishes to impart a unique umami flavor.

Lamb and goat are popular meats, often prepared in hearty stews like "Lamb Stew with Artichokes." This dish combines tender meat with the earthy taste of artichokes, creating a delightful and filling meal. Additionally, "Zuppa Gallurese" is a layered dish resembling lasagna, but instead of pasta, it features layers of bread soaked in broth and cheese.

Sardinia's desserts are equally enticing. "Sebadas" is a sweet treat consisting of deep-fried pastry filled with warm cheese and drizzled with honey. This combination of flavors creates a harmonious contrast between the savory and sweet elements. Another dessert, "Amaretti," are almond cookies often enjoyed with a glass of "Mirto," a local liqueur made from myrtle berries.

In Sardinian culture, meals are often a communal affair, emphasizing togetherness and celebration. Many traditional dishes have been passed down through generations, preserving the island's culinary heritage. The cuisine's reliance on simple, high-quality ingredients underscores the importance of the island's natural bounty.

In conclusion, traditional Sardinian dishes are a testament to the island's rich history, geographical diversity, and cultural values. From hearty meats to flavorful seafood and delightful desserts, Sardinian cuisine offers a journey through time and taste, allowing both locals and visitors to savor the essence of this unique Mediterranean gem.

9.4. STREET FOOD AND MARKETS

Sardinia, an Italian island known for its stunning landscapes and rich culture, offers a unique culinary experience through its vibrant street food and markets. The island's traditional flavors come alive in these bustling hubs, showcasing a blend of influences from Italian, Mediterranean, and even Spanish cuisines.

One of the standout street food options in Sardinia is "Pane Frattau." This dish features layers of thin flatbread soaked in tomato sauce and topped with poached eggs and grated Pecorino cheese. Another popular choice is "Supplì," a deep-fried rice ball stuffed with ragù, mozzarella, and sometimes saffron for added flavor.

Sardinian markets are a treasure trove for food enthusiasts. The "Mercato di San Benedetto" in Cagliari is a sprawling market offering an array of seafood, including the island's famed bottarga (cured fish roe) and freshly caught fish. The "Mercato di Testaccio" in Olbia is known for its vibrant colors and variety of local produce, such as artichokes, figs, and cheeses.

If you're looking for a taste of Sardinian cheese, head to the "Mercato Civico" in Nuoro. Here, you can find the famous Pecorino cheese, made from sheep's milk, in various aged varieties, each with a distinct flavor profile.

For those seeking a sensory overload, the "Mercato di Oristano" is a must-visit. This market offers a blend of food, clothing, and crafts, allowing you to immerse yourself in the local culture while savoring Sardinian delicacies.

Seafood lovers will relish the "Mercato Ittico" in Alghero, where the morning catch is displayed in all its glory. Indulge in fresh fish, octopus, and squid, either grilled or used as the star ingredient in traditional seafood stews.

No exploration of Sardinian street food and markets is complete without mentioning the "Pane Carasau," a thin, crispy flatbread often referred to as "music paper bread." It's a versatile staple that can be enjoyed on its own or used as a vessel for various toppings, both savory and sweet.

In conclusion, Sardinia's street food and markets offer a delightful journey into the island's culinary heritage. From savory treats like Pane Frattau and Supplì to the diverse selection of cheeses and seafood found in bustling markets, every bite in Sardinia is a celebration of flavor and culture. These culinary hubs provide an opportunity not only to taste the island's traditional dishes but also to engage with locals, immerse oneself in the vibrant atmosphere, and take home a piece of Sardinian gastronomy.

9.5. DIETARY PREFERENCES AND ALTERNATIVES

Sardinia, an Italian island known for its rich cultural heritage and stunning landscapes, also boasts a unique culinary scene deeply rooted in its history and geography. Dietary preferences in Sardinia are influenced by both tradition and availability of local ingredients. The island's cuisine reflects a blend of Mediterranean flavors, showcasing an array of alternatives for various dietary needs.

One of the prominent dietary preferences in Sardinia is the Mediterranean diet, which emphasizes whole foods like fruits, vegetables, legumes, whole grains, and olive oil. Seafood holds a special place due to its proximity to the Mediterranean Sea. Fresh fish such as anchovies, tuna, and sardines are commonly enjoyed. Locally produced cheeses like pecorino, made from sheep's milk, are a staple.

Sardinians also have a taste for meat, with dishes like "porceddu" (roast piglet) and "agnello" (lamb) being popular. However, the island's hilly terrain means that dairy and meat consumption is often lower compared to other regions in Italy. Instead, Sardinians rely on alternatives like legumes and grains for sustenance. "Fregula," a type of semolina pasta similar to couscous, is frequently used in soups and stews.

In recent years, dietary preferences have diversified to accommodate various lifestyles. Vegetarian and vegan options are becoming more available in response to growing global trends. Restaurants in Sardinia now offer plant-based alternatives such as pasta dishes with tomato and basil, eggplant parmigiana, and salads featuring local produce.

Gluten-free alternatives have also gained traction in Sardinia. Local grains like barley, farro, and corn are used to create gluten-free pasta, bread, and desserts. This is particularly significant given the prevalence of celiac disease and gluten sensitivities.

Sardinia's culinary culture is also characterized by its emphasis on seasonality and locality. The island's inhabitants have a strong connection to the land, often cultivating their own fruits, vegetables, and herbs. This practice ensures access to fresh, organic ingredients that are central to the island's dietary choices.

In conclusion, dietary preferences in Sardinia are deeply tied to its historical, geographical, and cultural influences. The Mediterranean diet serves as a foundation, with an abundance of seafood, dairy, and grains. However, the island's culinary landscape has evolved to accommodate modern dietary trends, offering options for vegetarians, vegans, and those with dietary restrictions. With an unwavering focus on fresh, local, and seasonal ingredients, Sardinia continues to provide a diverse array of alternatives to cater to various tastes and nutritional needs.

CHAPTER 10

SHOPPING AND SOUVENIRS

10.1. LOCAL MARKETS AND CRAFTSMANSHIP

Sardinia, a picturesque island nestled in the Mediterranean Sea, boasts a rich tradition of local markets and craftsmanship that are deeply intertwined with its cultural heritage. These markets, often referred to as "mercati" in Italian, serve as vibrant hubs where local artisans, farmers, and producers come together to showcase their products, creating a sensory feast for visitors and residents alike.

At these local markets, one can find a captivating array of goods that reflect the island's history and craftsmanship. Sardinia's artisanal traditions are rooted in its ancient past, with techniques passed down through generations. Intricate handwoven textiles, such as "tappeti sardi" (Sardinian carpets)

183

and "filet" lace, demonstrate the island's mastery of weaving and needlework. The vibrant colors and geometric patterns often found in these textiles are a testament to the island's unique aesthetic.

Another highlight of Sardinia's markets is the display of ceramics, a craft dating back to the Nuragic civilization that once inhabited the island. Artisans meticulously handcraft ceramics, creating stunning pieces adorned with traditional motifs and designs. These ceramics not only serve as functional items but also as exquisite works of art that capture the essence of Sardinia's history and natural beauty.

The markets also offer a bounty of agricultural products that showcase the island's fertile land and dedication to sustainable practices. Locally grown produce, such as aromatic herbs, succulent fruits, and unique varieties of cheese, provide a true taste of Sardinian cuisine. Additionally, the markets often feature local wines, including the renowned Cannonau red wine, which is produced from indigenous grape varieties and reflects the island's terroir.

Beyond the products themselves, Sardinia's markets are essential for fostering a sense of community and preserving cultural identity. The markets provide a space for artisans and producers to connect with consumers on a personal level, sharing stories and traditions behind their creations. This direct interaction adds depth to the shopping experience, making it a cultural journey rather than a mere transaction.

In recent years, efforts have been made to sustain and revitalize these markets. Local governments and organizations recognize the value of preserving traditional craftsmanship and promoting local economies. Festivals celebrating traditional crafts and local products have gained popularity, drawing both locals and tourists to these vibrant gatherings.

In essence, Sardinia's local markets and craftsmanship encapsulate the island's soul, echoing its storied past and vibrant present. The intricate textiles, masterful ceramics, flavorful produce, and warm community interactions all contribute to an experience that is both immersive and enlightening. As visitors stroll through these markets, they become not just spectators, but participants in a centuries-old tradition that continues to shape the cultural landscape of Sardinia.

10.2. TRADITIONAL TEXTILES AND CLOTHING

Traditional textiles and clothing in Sardinia have a rich history that reflects the island's cultural diversity and unique heritage. The island's geographical location in the Mediterranean has exposed it to various influences, resulting in a distinct and diverse range of textiles and garments.

One of the most iconic elements of Sardinian traditional clothing is the "traje," a term used to describe the elaborate folk costumes worn by locals during festive occasions. These costumes vary from region to region on the island, showcasing the distinctiveness of each area's culture. The traje typically consists of intricately woven fabrics, vibrant colors, and elaborate embroidery, often adorned with silver jewelry, buttons, and other accessories.

Wool has been a fundamental material in Sardinian textiles due to the island's historical sheep-rearing tradition. The intricate art of hand-weaving is a crucial aspect of Sardinia's textile heritage, with women playing a central role in this craft. They use traditional wooden looms to create fabrics like "tapis," which are intricately woven rugs featuring geometric patterns and vibrant hues.

One remarkable textile tradition is "filet lace," a technique that produces delicate and intricate lacework often used to embellish clothing, household items, and religious artifacts. This technique requires skillful craftsmanship, with lace-makers meticulously creating patterns by knotting and looping threads.

Sardinia's traditional clothing also includes unique accessories like the "pibiones," which are decorative buttons crafted from silver or other metals. These buttons are used to fasten garments and are often passed down through generations as heirlooms.

The island's history of trade and interaction with neighboring cultures, including Phoenicians, Romans, and Byzantines, has left a lasting impact on its textile traditions. These influences can be seen in the motifs, patterns, and techniques used in Sardinian textiles.

Despite modernization and changing fashion trends, efforts are being made to preserve and promote

Sardinia's traditional textiles and clothing. Local artisans and organizations strive to pass down the knowledge of weaving, lace-making, and embroidery to younger generations through workshops and cultural events.

In conclusion, Sardinia's traditional textiles and clothing are a testament to its rich history and cultural diversity. The intricate craftsmanship, vibrant colors, and unique designs of Sardinian textiles and garments reflect the island's deep-rooted traditions and the creativity of its people. Preserving and celebrating these traditions not only honors the island's past but also contributes to its cultural identity in the modern world.

10.3. CERAMIC WARE AND POTTERY

Ceramic ware and pottery in Sardinia have a rich and intricate history that spans centuries. This Mediterranean island, known for its unique culture, has been a hub of ceramic production since ancient times. Sardinian pottery is celebrated for its distinctive styles, intricate designs, and remarkable craftsmanship.

The tradition of creating ceramic ware in Sardinia dates back to the prehistoric Nuragic civilization, which flourished on the island from around 1800 to 238 BCE. These early inhabitants crafted pottery for utilitarian purposes such as cooking, storage, and religious rituals. The Nuragic pottery featured distinctive shapes and decorations, often showcasing geometric patterns and stylized representations of animals and humans.

As time progressed, Sardinian pottery evolved under the influence of various civilizations, including the Phoenicians, Carthaginians, Romans, Byzantines, and Moors. Each of these cultures left its mark on the island's ceramic traditions, resulting in a diverse range of styles and techniques.

One notable type of Sardinian pottery is "graffito" ware, characterized by its incised patterns and designs. Another prominent style is "Terra Sigillata Sarda," a red glazed pottery inspired by the Roman terra sigillata, but with a local flair. Additionally, the village of San Sperate is renowned for its colorful and artistic ceramics, often adorned with whimsical and imaginative motifs.

Today, Sardinian ceramic artisans continue to preserve these age-old techniques while incorporating modern elements to meet contemporary needs and tastes. The island's pottery industry plays a crucial role in both cultural preservation and economic sustainability, attracting tourists and collectors alike.

In conclusion, ceramic ware and pottery in Sardinia represent a captivating fusion of history, culture, and artistry. The island's ceramics not only offer insight into its past civilizations but also serve as a testament to the enduring creativity of its people.

With its unique styles and techniques passed down through generations, Sardinian pottery remains a testament to the island's rich cultural heritage.

10.4. SARDINIAN WINES AND FOOD PRODUCTS

Sardinia, an Italian island in the Mediterranean, boasts a rich culinary tradition with a focus on locally sourced ingredients and distinctive flavors. Sardinian wines and food products hold a special place in the island's culture and are celebrated both locally and internationally.

Sardinian wines have gained recognition for their unique character and exceptional quality. The island's diverse terroir, with its varied soils and climates, contributes to the production of a wide range of wines. One of the most renowned Sardinian wines is Cannonau, made from the Grenache grape. It's known for its robust and full-bodied nature, often compared to red wines from other Mediterranean regions. Vermentino is another popular varietal, yielding crisp and aromatic white wines that pair wonderfully with seafood, a staple in Sardinian cuisine.

Speaking of food, Sardinian cuisine is deeply rooted in tradition and showcases the island's agricultural richness. Pecorino cheese holds a significant place in Sardinian gastronomy. The island produces various types of Pecorino, each with its own aging process and distinct flavor profile. Casu Marzu, a traditional Sardinian cheese, is infamous for its unique preparation involving live insect larvae.

Sardinian bread, particularly pane carasau, is a thin and crispy flatbread that can be stored for months. It was traditionally used by shepherds during long journeys. Another iconic food is culurgiones, handmade pasta stuffed with fillings like potato, mint, and cheese, often served with tomato sauce.

Seafood is fundamental to Sardinian cuisine due to the island's coastal location. Dishes like fregola con arselle (pearl-like pasta with clams) and bottarga (cured fish roe) exemplify the use of marine ingredients in local cooking.

Sardinia's cuisine is characterized by its reliance on simple yet flavorful ingredients, often prepared in ways that have been passed down through generations. The island's wines and food products are a testament to its rich history, cultural diversity, and the natural bounty that its land and waters provide. Whether it's a hearty Cannonau paired with succulent roast meat or a plate of pasta adorned with freshly grated Pecorino, Sardinian wines and food products offer a tantalizing journey into the island's culinary soul.

10.5. Unique Souvenirs to Bring Home

Sardinia, the stunning Mediterranean island known for its pristine beaches, rich history, and unique culture, offers a plethora of distinctive souvenirs that make for cherished mementos of your visit. Here are some captivating options to consider bringing home:

1. Coral Jewelry: Sardinia is renowned for its coral jewelry, particularly the deep red variety found off its shores. Traditional craftsmanship transforms this coral into exquisite necklaces, earrings, and bracelets that showcase the island's marine beauty.

2. Sardinian Ceramics: Hand-painted ceramics from Sardinia display intricate designs and vibrant colors. You can find a variety of items like plates, tiles, and decorative pieces that reflect the island's artistic heritage.

3. Carved Wooden Artifacts: Skilled artisans create intricately carved wooden items, including masks, chests, and utensils. These pieces offer a glimpse into Sardinia's rural traditions and craftsmanship.

4. Bottarga: A culinary delight, bottarga is salted, cured fish roe, typically from mullet. This Sardinian specialty is often grated over pasta, imparting a unique and intense flavor. It's a wonderful edible souvenir.

5. Sheepskin Rugs and Textiles: Given the island's strong pastoral heritage, sheepskin rugs, blankets, and textiles are common souvenirs. These products not only represent Sardinia's rural life but also offer warmth and comfort.

6. Sardinian Wines: Sardinia boasts a rich winemaking tradition. Consider bringing home a bottle of Cannonau, a local red wine with a robust flavor profile, or the crisp white Vermentino. Wine enthusiasts will appreciate these distinctive selections.

7. Sardinian Knives: Sardinian knives, known as "Resolzas" or "Sardinian Knives," are crafted with precision and skill. They are often adorned with unique designs on their handles, making them functional pieces of art.

8. Traditional Costumes: While not the most practical souvenir, traditional Sardinian costumes exemplify the island's cultural heritage. Intricately embroidered and colorful, these costumes offer a visual representation of local festivities.

9. Local Cheeses: Sardinia produces a variety of distinctive cheeses, such as Pecorino Sardo. These cheeses are made from sheep's milk and offer a taste of the island's authentic flavors.

10. Liquors and Liqueurs: Mirto, a Sardinian liqueur made from myrtle berries, is a popular choice. It comes in both red and white varieties and is often enjoyed as a digestif.

Incorporating any of these souvenirs into your collection will not only remind you of your Sardinian experience but also connect you to the island's rich cultural tapestry. Whether it's a piece of jewelry, a culinary delight, or a decorative item, each souvenir encapsulates a fragment of Sardinia's enchanting allure.

CHAPTER 11

NIGHTLIFE AND ENTERTAINMENT

11.1. COASTAL BARS AND CLUBS

Sardinia, renowned for its stunning coastline and vibrant nightlife, boasts a variety of coastal bars and clubs that offer unique experiences for locals and tourists alike.

1. Phi Beach: Nestled in the rocky cliffs of Costa Smeralda, Phi Beach is an open-air club renowned for its breathtaking sunset views. Relax on cushioned seating while sipping on cocktails, enjoying a blend of electronic beats and natural beauty.

2. Billionaire Porto Cervo: A legendary destination for the rich and famous, this upscale club offers luxurious beachfront lounging, an exclusive atmosphere, and world-class DJs playing a mix of house, hip-hop, and R&B.

3. Baja Sardinia: This coastal village houses numerous bars and clubs, with Ritual Club being a standout. With its Mediterranean-inspired design and vibrant dance floor, it offers a mix of live music and DJ performances.

4. Cala Luna: A unique spot located in the enchanting Golfo di Orosei, Cala Luna features a beachside bar where visitors can enjoy cocktails and local wines while taking in views of turquoise waters and limestone cliffs.

5. Cala Mariolu: Known for its crystal-clear waters, Cala Mariolu offers a laid-back beach bar scene. While not a traditional club, its natural beauty and relaxed vibe make it a must-visit spot for a tranquil beachside drink.

6. Cagliari Waterfront: The capital city's seafront promenade is lined with bars and clubs. Poetto Beach features several beachfront bars, like Lido and Nautilus, offering a mix of music, drinks, and sea views.

7. Alghero: Tucked into Sardinia's northwest corner, Alghero offers a mix of bars and clubs along its historic cobblestone streets. Sunset Lounge Bar stands out with its sea-facing terrace and live music.

8. Porto Pollo: This windsurfing and kiteboarding hub transforms into a lively party scene after sunset. Head to the beachside Tiki Bar to enjoy drinks and music with the backdrop of energetic water sports.

9. Spiaggia del Principe: Although not a club, this stunning beach features a kiosk where visitors can enjoy refreshments while relishing the unspoiled natural surroundings. The atmosphere is serene, making it perfect for a peaceful drink.

10. Villasimius: This town offers a mix of bars and clubs along its coastline. The Karibu Lounge Bar offers a relaxed setting with comfortable seating, sea views, and live music.

In these coastal bars and clubs of Sardinia, visitors can revel in a range of experiences, from high-end luxury to laid-back beach vibes. Whether you're dancing under the stars at Phi Beach or sipping cocktails by the sea at Cala Luna, each venue offers a distinct ambiance that captures the essence of Sardinia's coastal charm and vibrant nightlife.

11.2. LIVE MUSIC AND PERFORMANCES

Sardinia, a captivating Italian island known for its rich history and stunning landscapes, also boasts a vibrant live music and performance scene that reflects its unique cultural heritage. From traditional folk music to contemporary genres, Sardinia offers a diverse range of musical experiences that enchant both locals and visitors.

The island's traditional music is deeply rooted in its history and customs. "Cantu a tenore," a mesmerizing form of polyphonic singing, is a UNESCO-recognized intangible cultural heritage of humanity. This style, performed by groups of four men, involves intricate harmonies and distinctive vocal techniques. Additionally, the launeddas, a triple-reed instrument, is another hallmark of Sardinian traditional music, often used to accompany dances and rituals.

As for modern live music, Sardinia hosts various events and festivals throughout the year. The "Time in Jazz" festival in Berchidda, founded by renowned trumpeter Paolo Fresu, attracts international jazz artists and enthusiasts. Another highlight is the "Cavalcata Sarda" in Sassari, a celebration of Sardinian culture featuring colorful parades, traditional costumes, and live music performances.

Coastal towns and cities like Cagliari, Alghero, and Olbia also contribute to the island's musical vibrancy. Piazzas and squares come alive with buskers, street performers, and local bands, providing an inviting atmosphere for both residents and tourists to enjoy. Bars and clubs in these urban centers often host live bands spanning a range of genres, from rock and pop to electronic and experimental music.

Sardinia's outdoor venues are equally captivating. The Roman amphitheater in Cagliari occasionally hosts open-air concerts, infusing a touch of history into modern performances. Beachside stages in coastal areas offer unique opportunities to revel in music while surrounded by picturesque views.

In conclusion, Sardinia's live music and performance scene embody the island's deep cultural roots and artistic dynamism. Whether it's the hauntingly beautiful traditional music or the energetic modern performances, Sardinia provides a musical experience that resonates with the island's rich heritage and contemporary spirit.

11.3. CULTURAL EVENTS AND EXHIBITIONS

Sardinia, the picturesque Italian island known for its rich history and captivating landscapes, offers a vibrant array of cultural events and exhibitions that showcase its unique heritage. From traditional festivals to contemporary art displays, Sardinia's cultural scene provides a blend of old-world charm and modern creativity.

One of the most prominent events is the "Sagra di Sant'Efisio," a religious procession held annually on May 1st in Cagliari, the island's capital. This colorful event features locals dressed in traditional attire, parading through the streets to honor the patron saint of the city. The procession culminates at the Nora beach, where a stunning seafront ceremony takes place.

The "Cortes Apertas" event, which translates to "Open Courtyards," is a window into Sardinia's rural life. Held in various towns during the summer months, this event invites visitors to explore private courtyards, sample local cuisine, and witness traditional crafts like weaving and pottery-making. It's a unique opportunity to experience the island's authenticity.

For art enthusiasts, the "Festival Internazionale del Folklore" in Tempio Pausania is a must-visit. This festival brings together artists and performers from around the world to celebrate diverse cultures through music, dance, and traditional crafts. It's a testament to Sardinia's global outlook and appreciation for cultural exchange.

Sardinia also boasts several museums and galleries. The "Museo Archeologico Nazionale" in Cagliari houses an impressive collection of artifacts from prehistoric to Roman times, offering insights into the island's ancient civilizations. The "Museo MAN" in Nuoro focuses on Sardinian art and culture, featuring works by renowned local artists.

In the realm of contemporary art, the "Art Night" in Alghero stands out. This event transforms the historic town into an open-air gallery, with contemporary artworks displayed in the narrow streets and squares. It's a testament to Sardinia's ability to merge its historical backdrop with modern artistic expression.

Nature and culture intersect during the "Cavalcata Sarda" in Sassari, a festival that celebrates the island's strong connection to horsemanship. Locals dress in traditional costumes and parade on horseback, demonstrating their equestrian skills and paying homage to the island's rural heritage.

In conclusion, Sardinia's cultural events and exhibitions offer a captivating blend of tradition and modernity. From religious processions and open courtyard festivals to museums showcasing ancient artifacts and contemporary art installations, the island provides a diverse range of experiences that reflect its unique identity and rich history. Whether you're drawn to centuries-old customs or contemporary artistic expression, Sardinia's cultural scene has something to offer for every enthusiast.

11.4. TRADITIONAL MUSIC AND DANCE

Traditional music and dance in Sardinia, an enchanting Italian island in the Mediterranean Sea, are deeply rooted in its rich cultural heritage. These expressions serve as a window into the island's history, reflecting the influences of various civilizations that have shaped its identity over millennia.

Sardinian music is characterized by its unique vocal polyphony, often performed by male choirs known as "cuncordu" and "tenore." These harmonious melodies, accompanied by traditional instruments like the launeddas (a triple-piped reed instrument), capture the island's rustic charm and evoke a sense of connection to its pastoral landscapes.

The dances of Sardinia are equally captivating. The "ballu tundu" is a circular dance where participants hold hands and move gracefully to the rhythm of traditional instruments like the guitar, accordion, and violin. Another notable dance is the "su passu torrau," which involves intricate footwork and rhythmic patterns, demonstrating the islanders' strong connection to their land and history.

The costumes worn during these performances are a visual spectacle. Intricately designed, they vary from region to region on the island, showcasing the diversity of Sardinian culture. Women often wear colorful dresses with elaborate embroidery, while men don traditional attire like the "giponu" and "berritta."

These musical and dance traditions hold significance beyond mere entertainment. They often accompany religious festivals, agricultural celebrations, and other communal events, reinforcing the island's social bonds and collective identity.

In recent times, efforts have been made to preserve and promote Sardinia's traditional music and dance. Festivals, workshops, and cultural centers have emerged to ensure that these artistic expressions continue to thrive, passing down the island's history and values to future generations.

In essence, Sardinia's traditional music and dance encapsulate the island's soul, offering a timeless glimpse into its past while celebrating the vibrant spirit of its people.

11.5. STARGAZING AND NIGHT TOURS

Stargazing and night tours in Sardinia offer an enchanting opportunity to explore the island's celestial wonders and nocturnal landscapes. Situated in the Mediterranean, Sardinia's relatively low levels of light pollution make it an ideal destination for avid astronomers and nature enthusiasts to delve into the mysteries of the night sky.

The island's diverse geography, encompassing pristine beaches, rugged mountains, and rolling hills, provides a captivating backdrop for night tours. Professional guides often lead these tours, offering their expertise on both the celestial and terrestrial aspects of the experience. Participants can embark on nocturnal hikes to vantage points that provide unobstructed views of the heavens, allowing them to witness constellations, planets, and shooting stars with unparalleled clarity.

One of the most sought-after events in Sardinia is the Perseid meteor shower, which peaks in August. During this celestial spectacle, streaks of light traverse the sky, creating a breathtaking display that can be enjoyed during organized stargazing events. These events frequently include informative talks on astronomy, enhancing participants' understanding of the celestial mechanics behind meteor showers and other astronomical phenomena.

Sardinia also boasts observatories equipped with state-of-the-art telescopes that offer an even closer look at distant galaxies, nebulas, and planets. Visitors can join guided observatory tours to observe celestial bodies that are otherwise obscured by light pollution in more urban areas. Knowledgeable astronomers lead discussions, unraveling the secrets of the cosmos and offering insight into the history of astronomy.

Beyond stargazing, night tours in Sardinia delve into the island's nocturnal ecosystem. Visitors have the opportunity to spot elusive wildlife that only emerges after dusk, such as owls, bats, and nocturnal mammals. Guided walks through forests and along coastal areas unveil a world that comes to life when the sun sets, showcasing the beauty and diversity of Sardinia's natural environment.

To make the most of the stargazing and night tour experience, it's recommended to plan ahead and check for local events or guided tours that align with your visit. Additionally, packing appropriately for nighttime excursions by wearing warm clothing, comfortable shoes, and bringing along a flashlight enhances the overall enjoyment of the adventure.

In conclusion, stargazing and night tours in Sardinia offer a captivating blend of astronomical wonder and natural exploration. With its pristine landscapes, limited light pollution, and knowledgeable guides, Sardinia provides an ideal setting for individuals eager to connect with the cosmos and witness the enchanting beauty of the night sky. Whether you're an astronomy enthusiast or simply looking to experience the island's nocturnal magic, Sardinia's stargazing and night tours are sure to leave an indelible impression.

CHAPTER 12

PRACTICAL INFORMATION

12.1. CURRENCY AND BANKING

Currency and banking in Sardinia have played a crucial role in the economic development and financial history of this Mediterranean island. Over the centuries, Sardinia has experienced various phases of currency use and banking practices, reflecting its changing political and economic landscape.

Historically, Sardinia was home to diverse civilizations, each with its own currency systems. Phoenicians, Romans, Byzantines, and later, various Italian states, have left their mark on Sardinian currency. In the Middle Ages, Sardinia witnessed a mix of currencies, including the gold florin, silver coins, and copper denari. This diversity reflected the island's political fragmentation.

During the Spanish and Habsburg periods, Sardinia was integrated into broader currency systems. The Spanish Escudo and the Austrian Thaler circulated widely. In the 18th century, the Kingdom of Sardinia established its own currency, the Sardinian lira, which continued through the early 19th century.

The modern era of currency and banking in Sardinia began with Italian unification in the mid-19th century. The lira became the official currency of the newly formed Kingdom of Italy. Sardinia's financial institutions aligned with those of the mainland, and the Banca d'Italia took over the role of issuing currency.

In the 20th century, Sardinia experienced economic changes that affected its banking landscape. Industrialization and tourism brought economic growth, leading to the establishment of local banks and credit cooperatives. These institutions facilitated the island's economic diversification and development.

Today, the Euro (adopted in 2002) serves as the official currency of Sardinia and the entire Eurozone. The island's banking sector is integrated into the broader European financial system, with major Italian banks having a presence in Sardinia. Local banks and credit unions continue to serve the island's population, offering a range of financial services.

The economic challenges faced by Sardinia, including unemployment and regional disparities, have prompted discussions on how the banking sector can contribute to its development. Efforts have been made to promote local entrepreneurship and innovation through specialized financial services. Additionally, sustainable banking practices have gained prominence, aligning with global trends toward environmental and social responsibility.

In conclusion, currency and banking in Sardinia have evolved significantly over time, reflecting the island's historical, political, and economic changes. From the diverse ancient currencies to the modern adoption of the Euro, Sardinia's financial landscape has played a pivotal role in its economic trajectory. As the island continues to navigate economic challenges, its banking sector remains vital for fostering growth and addressing regional disparities.

12.2. SAFETY TIPS AND EMERGENCY CONTACTS

Sardinia, known for its stunning landscapes and rich history, offers a wonderful travel experience. To ensure your safety during your visit, it's essential to be aware of a few key safety tips and emergency contacts.

1. Health Precautions: Carry essential medications and a small first aid kit. Stay hydrated, especially during hot summer months. Apply sunscreen to protect against strong sun rays.

2. Natural Hazards: While exploring Sardinia's natural beauty, be cautious of uneven terrain, especially in rocky areas and hilly trails. Keep a safe distance from cliffs and always follow designated paths.

3. Swimming Safety: Sardinia boasts gorgeous beaches, but currents can be strong. Only swim in designated swimming areas, and heed any warning flags. Keep an eye on the sea conditions and never underestimate the power of the waves.

4. Local Laws and Customs: Familiarize yourself with local laws and customs to avoid any misunderstandings. Public nudity is not accepted, and smoking is prohibited in indoor public spaces.

5. Transportation Safety: If you're renting a car or scooter, follow local traffic rules. Roads can be winding and narrow, so drive carefully. Use seat belts at all times and avoid using your phone while driving.

6. Emergency Numbers:
- Police: 112
- Medical Emergency: 118
- Fire Department: 115
- Coast Guard: 1530

7. Language: While English is spoken in tourist areas, it's helpful to know some basic Italian phrases. This can aid in communication during emergencies or when seeking assistance.

8. Cultural Sensitivity: Respect local customs and traditions. When attending churches or other places of worship, dress modestly.

9. Wildlife Caution: Sardinia is home to various wildlife species. While encounters are rare, maintain a safe distance and avoid feeding any animals you may come across.

10. Emergency Plan: Before setting out on your adventures, share your itinerary with a trusted friend or family member. Keep your phone charged and have a backup charger ready.

Remember that while Sardinia is generally safe, unexpected situations can arise. By staying informed, practicing caution, and being prepared, you can make the most of your trip while ensuring your safety.

12.3. LOCAL ETIQUETTE AND CUSTOMS

Sardinia, an enchanting island in the Mediterranean, boasts a rich cultural tapestry woven with unique customs and traditions. Navigating its local etiquette can enhance your experience. Hospitality is paramount here, and guests are often warmly received with a kiss on both cheeks. Engaging in small talk before getting to business is customary, as relationships are highly valued.

Dining customs reflect Sardinia's communal spirit. During meals, pace yourself, as Sardinians savor their food. It's customary to finish everything on your plate, a sign of appreciation. Don't be surprised if you're offered second helpings – declining may be seen as impolite.

When visiting religious sites or attending events, conservative attire is recommended. Sardinians hold their traditions close, particularly in rural areas. Taking photographs during religious ceremonies or inside churches might be frowned upon.

Festivals are integral to Sardinian life. The "Sagra" food festivals celebrate local cuisine, and the "Cavalcata Sarda" features a vibrant parade with traditional costumes and music. Joining in with enthusiasm is a fantastic way to embrace the local culture.

Engaging in conversations about Sardinia's history, particularly its distinct language and past struggles, shows genuine interest and respect for the island's identity. Learning a few phrases in Sardinian, a Romance language, can earn you locals' admiration.

Beach etiquette is crucial due to Sardinia's stunning coastline. Always use a towel or beach mat, as sand cleanliness is appreciated. Topless sunbathing is generally acceptable, but nude sunbathing is reserved for designated areas.

When shopping, remember that most stores close during the afternoon "siesta" hours. As a sign of courtesy, greet shopkeepers when entering a store and when leaving.

Tipping in Sardinia isn't obligatory, as a service charge is often included in bills. However, leaving a small tip is appreciated. Rounding up the bill or leaving spare change is a common practice.

Lastly, respecting local customs includes protecting the environment. Sardinia's natural beauty is a point of pride, and littering is highly frowned upon. Dispose of your waste properly to show your appreciation for the island's splendor.

In essence, Sardinia's etiquette and customs are a reflection of its people's strong sense of community, history, and reverence for nature. By embracing these traditions, you'll undoubtedly create meaningful connections and lasting memories on this captivating island.

12.4. INTERNET AND COMMUNICATION

Sardinia, an Italian island in the Mediterranean, has seen significant advancements in internet and communication technologies in recent years. While it's known for its stunning landscapes and rich history, its digital infrastructure has also been evolving.

The island's internet connectivity has improved, with both urban and rural areas benefiting from increased broadband access. Telecommunication companies have been expanding their networks, offering higher speeds and better coverage. This has facilitated better communication for residents, businesses, and tourists.

Mobile communication has become seamless in Sardinia, with widespread 4G coverage and the ongoing deployment of 5G networks. This has enhanced mobile internet speeds and enabled the use of data-intensive applications on the go.

Sardinia's tourism industry has also leveraged technology to connect with visitors. Many accommodations, restaurants, and tourist attractions offer Wi-Fi access, enhancing the overall travel experience. Additionally, digital platforms and social media play a vital role in promoting local culture, events, and destinations to a global audience.

However, challenges persist. Remote and less populated areas still face occasional connectivity issues, hindering equal access to the benefits of the digital age. Efforts are being made to bridge this gap through government initiatives and private investments.

In conclusion, Sardinia has made remarkable strides in internet and communication infrastructure. From improved broadband access to the rollout of 5G, these developments have positively impacted various aspects of life on the island, including business, tourism, and local connectivity. Nonetheless, ensuring equitable access across all regions remains an ongoing objective.

12.5. ESSENTIAL SERVICES AND FACILITIES

Sardinia, a picturesque island in the Mediterranean Sea, offers a range of essential services and facilities to cater to its residents and visitors. From healthcare to transportation, the island ensures a comfortable and convenient experience for all.

Healthcare services on the island are well-established, with numerous hospitals, clinics, and medical centers spread across various towns. The island boasts a comprehensive network of healthcare professionals, including doctors, nurses, and specialists, ensuring that both routine and emergency medical needs are met efficiently.

Sardinia's transportation infrastructure includes a mix of options. An extensive road network connects different regions, making travel by car convenient. The island also has a reliable public transportation system consisting of buses and trains, connecting major towns and even remote areas. The Cagliari

Elmas Airport serves as the main gateway for domestic and international flights, ensuring smooth connectivity.

Education is a priority in Sardinia, with schools providing quality education at all levels. From preschools to universities, the island offers a diverse range of educational institutions. This ensures that residents have access to learning opportunities that align with their preferences and goals.

For those seeking relaxation and leisure, Sardinia's stunning beaches are complemented by a range of hospitality services. Hotels, resorts, and vacation rentals offer various accommodation options, catering to different budgets and preferences. The island's culinary scene is equally vibrant, with restaurants serving local delicacies and international cuisine.

Public safety is upheld through law enforcement agencies, ensuring a secure environment for residents and tourists alike. Sardinia's police force maintains a visible presence across the island, contributing to a sense of safety and well-being.

Sardinia's utility services, including water, electricity, and waste management, are efficiently managed, ensuring a comfortable living environment. These services are typically reliable and well-maintained, contributing to the overall quality of life on the island.

Cultural and recreational facilities abound in Sardinia, catering to various interests. Museums, art galleries, and cultural centers celebrate the island's rich history and heritage. Outdoor enthusiasts can explore national parks, hiking trails, and water sports opportunities.

In conclusion, Sardinia provides a comprehensive range of essential services and facilities that contribute to a high quality of life for its residents and an enjoyable experience for visitors. From healthcare and education to transportation and leisure, the island's offerings are designed to meet diverse needs and preferences.

CONCLUSION

Sardinia stands as a multifaceted gem, captivating travelers with its diverse offerings and enchanting landscapes. This Mediterranean island, with its unique blend of history, culture, and natural beauty, has undoubtedly proven itself to be a destination worthy of exploration. Throughout this travel guide, we have delved into the island's myriad attractions, unveiling the treasures that await those who venture to its shores.

From the sun-kissed beaches that fringe its coastline to the rugged mountain ranges that cut through its heart, Sardinia's geographical diversity is a testament to nature's artistry. Whether it's the allure of the Costa Smeralda, famed for its azure waters and luxury resorts, or the untamed wilderness of Gennargentu National Park, the island caters to every kind of traveler's wanderlust.

Delving deeper, we have uncovered Sardinia's rich history, a tapestry woven by various civilizations that have left their indelible marks. The ancient nuragic structures, mysterious stone towers that dot the landscape, stand as silent sentinels of a bygone era. The Phoenicians, Romans, and Byzantines have all played their part in shaping the island's cultural mosaic, which is still evident in its architecture, cuisine, and festivals.

Speaking of cuisine, Sardinia's gastronomic scene is a revelation in itself. From the simple yet flavorful pane frattau to the hearty and savory porceddu, each dish is a testament to the islanders' love for their land and its bounties. The generous use of locally sourced ingredients reflects not only the island's agricultural heritage but also its commitment to preserving tradition.

However, it's the warmth and authenticity of the Sardinian people that truly leave an indelible impression. Their hospitality, steeped in centuries-old customs, welcomes visitors as if they were old friends. Engaging with locals offers an intimate glimpse into daily life, and perhaps a taste of the Sardinian spirit that makes the island so endearing.

As travelers navigate through the pages of this guide, they're encouraged to not just scratch the surface but to immerse themselves in all that Sardinia has to offer. Whether it's exploring the charming cobblestone streets of Alghero's old town, embarking on a journey into the past at the archaeological sites, or simply basking in the tranquility of a secluded cove, Sardinia invites exploration at every turn.

In conclusion, Sardinia's allure lies not only in its stunning vistas and historical marvels but also in the emotions it evokes and the memories it creates. This travel guide has endeavored to capture the essence of the island, but the true magic of Sardinia can only be fully grasped through personal experience.

As you embark on your journey to this captivating island, may you discover its hidden corners, forge connections with its people, and create your own narrative amid its breathtaking landscapes. Sardinia beckons – a treasure trove of experiences and a realm where every moment is a postcard-worthy memory waiting to be lived.

FINAL TIPS AND RECOMMENDATIONS

Sardinia, the gem of the Mediterranean, promises an enchanting travel experience with its pristine beaches, rich history, and captivating culture. As you embark on your journey to this Italian paradise, here are some final tips and recommendations to ensure your Sardinian adventure is nothing short of extraordinary.

1. Diverse Exploration: Sardinia is a diverse playground for nature enthusiasts and history buffs alike. From the surreal beauty of Costa Smeralda's turquoise waters to the ancient ruins of Nora and

Tharros, each corner has a unique story to tell. Make sure to explore both the coastline and the rugged interior to fully appreciate the island's beauty.

2. Culinary Delights: Sardinia's cuisine is a reflection of its unique heritage. Don't miss the chance to savor its traditional dishes like "porceddu" (suckling pig) and "malloreddus" (Sardinian gnocchi). Pair your meals with local wines like Cannonau and Vermentino for an authentic experience that tantalizes your taste buds.

3. Beach Bliss: With its breathtaking beaches, Sardinia is a haven for sun seekers. The Costa Rei, La Pelosa, and Cala Goloritzé are just a few of the countless stretches of powdery sand and crystalline waters that beckon you to relax and unwind.

4. Local Etiquette: Embrace the warmth of Sardinian hospitality by familiarizing yourself with local customs. A simple "buongiorno" (good morning) or "grazie" (thank you) in Italian can go a long way in building connections with the locals.

5. Festivals and Traditions: Immerse yourself in Sardinia's vibrant traditions by timing your visit with one of its many festivals. The spectacular "Sartiglia" horse race in Oristano or the "Cavalcata Sarda" in Sassari offer a glimpse into the island's rich cultural heritage.

6. Island of Nuraghi: Explore the mystical Nuragic civilization, unique to Sardinia. The Nuraghe Su Nuraxi in Barumini is a UNESCO World Heritage site and provides insight into an ancient culture that once thrived on the island.

7. Pack Smart: Depending on the season, pack comfortable clothing, sunscreen, a hat, and sturdy footwear for exploring both urban centers and natural wonders. Sardinia's weather can be unpredictable, so be prepared for sudden changes.

8. Transportation: While renting a car gives you the freedom to explore, Sardinia also boasts an efficient public transportation system. Ferries are crucial for island hopping, so plan your routes in advance.

9. Language Basics: While many locals speak English, a few Italian phrases can enhance your experience. Learning a few words can show your respect for the local culture.

10. Respect Nature: Sardinia's beauty is fragile. As you venture into its natural wonders, practice responsible tourism by leaving no trace and adhering to conservation guidelines.

From its rugged landscapes to its warm-hearted inhabitants, Sardinia casts a spell that lingers long after you've left its shores. By embracing the island's culture, history, and natural splendor, you'll undoubtedly create memories that will stay with you forever. So, pack your sense of adventure and get ready for an unforgettable journey through this Mediterranean paradise.

ADDITIONAL RESOURCES

When planning a trip to Sardinia, there are several additional resources that can enhance your travel experience beyond a traditional guidebook:

1. Travel Blogs and Websites: Explore personal travel blogs and websites that offer first-hand accounts, insider tips, and detailed itineraries from travelers who have visited Sardinia. These platforms provide a more authentic and up-to-date perspective on local attractions, hidden gems, and practical travel advice.

2. Online Forums and Communities: Engage with online travel forums and communities dedicated to Sardinia. Platforms like TripAdvisor, Reddit, or Lonely Planet's Thorn Tree allow you to ask questions, seek recommendations, and interact with other travelers who have been to or are planning to visit the island.

3. Social Media: Follow travel influencers, photographers, and travel-related accounts on platforms like Instagram. You'll find stunning visuals of Sardinia's landscapes, culture, and cuisine. These images can inspire your itinerary and give you a glimpse of what to expect.

4. Local Blogs and News Websites: Explore local blogs and news websites from Sardinia. These sources can provide insights into current events, festivals, and cultural happenings. They're valuable for understanding the local context and immersing yourself in the island's culture.

5. YouTube: Watch travel vlogs and videos showcasing Sardinia. Video content can provide a more dynamic understanding of the destination, allowing you to virtually explore attractions, local markets, and activities.

6. Travel Apps: Download apps that offer offline maps, local transportation information, and language translation tools. These apps can be invaluable for navigating Sardinia's streets, finding restaurants, and communicating with locals.

7. Cookbooks and Food Blogs: If you're interested in Sardinian cuisine, consider exploring cookbooks and food blogs that highlight traditional recipes and culinary experiences. This can be a great way to connect with the local culture through food.

8. Historical and Cultural Resources: Delve into books, documentaries, or online resources that delve into Sardinia's history, traditions, and cultural heritage. Understanding the background of the place can make your visit more meaningful.

Remember that while these resources can provide valuable insights, they should be used to supplement, not replace, the information found in guidebooks. Combining various sources will ensure a comprehensive and well-rounded travel experience in Sardinia.

Printed in Great Britain
by Amazon

38269020R00134